Under five – under-educated?

Under five – under-educated?

Tricia David

Open University Press
Milton Keynes · Philadelphia

Open University Press
Celtic Court
22 Ballmoor
Buckingham MK18 1XW

and
1900 Frost Road, Suite 101
Bristol, PA 19007, USA

First Published 1990

British Library Catloguing in Publication Data
David, Tricia
    Under five – Under-educated?
    1. Pre-School children. Education
    I. Title
    372′.21

    ISBN 0 335 09263 2
    ISBN 0 335 09262 4

Library of Congress Cataloging-in-Publication Data

David, Tricia, 1942-
        Under five – under-educated?/Tricia David
            p.   cm.
        Includes bibliographical references (p.).
        ISBN 0–335–09263–2—ISBN 0–335–09262–4
        1. Education, Preschool—Great Britain. 2. Education, Preschool
    Great Britain—Parent participation. I. Title.
    LB1140.25.G7D38   1990
    372.21′0941—dc20   89-48156CIP

Typeset by Gilbert Composing Services, Leighton Buzzard
Printed in Great Britain by J.W. Arrowsmith Ltd., Bristol

For Sacha and Ceris

Contents

List of abbreviations

AFFOR	All Faiths For One Race
BAECE	British Association for Early Childhood Education
CACE	Central Advisory Council for Education
CEDC	Community Education Development Centre
CERD	Centre for Educational Research and Development
CERI	Centre for Research and Innovation
CPAG	Child Poverty Action Group
CRC	Community Relations Commission
CRE	Commission for Racial Equality
CRER	Centre for Research in Ethnic Relations
DES	Department of Education and Science
DHSS	Department of Health and Social Security
EOC	Equal Opportunities Commission
EPA	educational priority area
HMI	Her Majesty's Inspectorate
ILEA	Inner London Education Authority
LEA	Local Education Authority
NAHT	National Association of Head Teachers
NAPE	National Association for Primary Education
NCB	National Children's Bureau
NCMA	National Childminders' Association
NCVO	National Council for Voluntary Organizations
NUT	National Union of Teachers
OMEP	Organisation Mondiale pour l'Education Préscolaire (World Organization for Preschool Education)
OPCS	Office of Population Censuses and Surveys
PPA	Preschool Playgroups Association

SAT   standard assessment task
TUC   Trades Union Congress
VOLCUF Voluntary Organizations Liaison Council for Under Fives
WEA   Workers' Education Association

Preface and acknowledgements

Almost fifteen years ago, when Dr Stephen Tyler and I were members of the research group of Keele University Psychology Department, we decided to write a book together about the education of preschool children. Many events during the intervening years caused us to postpone our plan, the saddest being the death of Dr Corinne Hutt, to whom we both owe so much. However, the greatest barrier to our collaboration on this project has been the workload we have both encountered, as we have moved on to other professional experiences. The book which has finally emerged is probably very different from our original idea, partly because of the research results of those fifteen years, partly because Stephen's other commitments forced him to withdraw from the enterprise and the work became solely my responsibility, partly because the economic climate and demographic situation now provide a context we would not have anticipated.

In writing a book of this kind, one becomes aware of both the near and distant contacts, through time and space, who have influenced one's own thoughts, feelings, hopes and learning. In my case the list is endless, stretching from the exciting and loving extended family with whom I spent my own preschool years in Manchester; through undergraduate study at Nottingham under the influence of Drs John and Elizabeth Newson; parenthood and life in France, where I observed different attitudes to young children from those widespread in Britain; the Staffordshire Preschool Playgroup Movement with friends like the late Dr Yvonne Lejeune who taught me so much; Professor John Hutt and the Keele University Preschool Research team; early childhood colleagues up and down the country, especially Miss Gwen Stubbs and Mrs Jenny Clement and others in Staffordshire, Warwickshire, Coventry and

Solihull; students and staff at Warwick University; to, perhaps most importantly, the very young children and their parents who have given me unending pleasure, affection and food for thought over the last quarter of a century.

Additionally, special thanks are due to Dr Ann Lewis, for reading and commenting so incisively on the manuscript; to John Skelton of Open University Press, for his extremely helpful editing; to Ann Ramsden, without whom I could not have completed the word-processing on time; to Jim Campbell for being a collegial (and congenial) mentor; and to Roy David, for his constant support, encouragement and sense of the absurd.

In this book I have tried to make clear the differences between types of provision where it is important to do so. On other occasions, the word 'nursery' or 'preschool' group may apply to any of the forms of provision, and, where adult workers are referred to, I hope childminders and home-based nannies will include themselves wherever appropriate. I have also endeavoured to use the now conventional ways of avoiding limiting, sexist language.

If some of the chapters seem overloaded with references to research and other literature, this has been a deliberate act on my part, not simply to support my view, or to refute someone else's, but to point readers to other more detailed work on the issues discussed.

SETTING THE SCENE

1
Introduction

The last ten years of the twentieth century may be crucial for two groups
in the United Kingdom. One of these groups, our youngest children, is
expected to rise to a peak in the mid-1990s (Family Policy Studies Centre,
1989), when it is anticipated there will be 4.1 million children under five,
half a million more than in 1986. The number is likely to fall again after
this, so that by the year 2025 the under-five population will be
approaching its level during the mid-1980s (3.6 million).

Women comprise the second group for whom the end of the twentieth
century is likely to be significant. The fall in the birthrate has meant that
the country will soon be desperately short of workers, and government
and employers are addressing the issue by suggesting that the proportion
of women in the workforce will need to increase in order to maintain the
country's economic viability.

Currently (OPCS, 1989), more than half of all the women in the UK
aged 16–59, who have dependent children, are economically active, yet
the greatest proportion of these are in part-time work, owing to the lack
of facilities for preschoolers, or care for older children outside school
hours. As one would expect, the number of women employed outside the
home is lowest for the group who have the youngest children.

Recent work by Pugh (1988), Cohen (1988) and Moss (1988) has
indicated the patchy and unfair nature of preschool provision. In the
absence of a national policy, local authorities have developed services in
response to economic and political factors, rather than basing their
actions on the needs and democratic rights of those concerned.

An additional strand in the situation is the implementation of a
National Curriculum (DES, 1987) for children of statutory school age
(5–16 years). This new enforcement is believed necessary both for the

raising of standards of achievement in the population and as an entitlement for all children. The programmes of study were incorporated into the work of schools in September 1989.

The lives of our youngest children and those of their parents are inextricably bound together. Further, as life is currently lived in the UK, in most cases it is the mother, even when she has a partner, who makes most adjustments to her life with the arrival of children. The majority of women who must make such adjustments do so with pleasure, or at least with responsible resignation. Some are adamant that they will remain out of the workforce until their children are old enough to be fairly independent, but feel there are pressures on them from society to do otherwise. These pressures are likely to grow during the early 1990s, particularly if they are women with a special skill to offer.

Some women may be in a position to work from home, and it will be a measure of our development as a society respecting individual rights if such women are paid fairly rather than being subjected to the usual exploitation experienced by women home workers.

The ideology of the family and the lack of any commitment on the part of successive governments to high-quality preschool facilities has led the majority of mothers of young children who do work outside the home to accept part-time employment. In itself this might appear an admirable solution, since it is possible the mothers wish to spend part of the day with their children. However, these women form another large group of workers who are vulnerable and easily exploited by some less scrupulous employers, although it could be argued that this is all part of what a market economy means.

The contradiction between the present Conservative government's espoused ideal of family life and its recognition that the economy will fail if women are not enticed into the labour force is proving a difficult issue to handle. A Women's Issues Group of representatives from the different government departments has been set up, and employers and others, such as the preschool playgroup movement, are being encouraged to explore ways of making care facilities available. In addition, a Committee of Inquiry has been set up by the government, following the publication of the House of Commons Select Committee (1989) Report, to investigate ways in which the education of children under five can be developed without spending any more money than is currently available. Local authorities are being told that any increases in childcare facilities on the rates – or rather, on the Community Charge (poll tax) – is their responsibility and nothing to do with central government.

Around 75 per cent of four-year-olds are in maintained schools (either nursery or reception classes) but there are very few facilities, other than family members, friends or childminders, to look after these children before or after the school day. There has also been grave concern about the kind of provision the majority of these four-year-olds, those in the primary school reception classes, are experiencing.

The fact that some provision focuses on education, with the involvement of qualified teachers, while other establishments are labelled 'care' because they do not, or because they are not administered by LEAs, has led to confusion for parents and rivalries among the providers. Given a choice, most parents stated (Bone, 1977) that they would want nursery school or class provision for their under-fives and the survey of research by Clark (1988) supports the view that the involvement of teachers in provision for nursery children is essential. However, given the current shortage of teachers wishing to work in maintained schools, we may see an increase in the number of nurseries deprived of their teachers because they have been forcibly redeployed in the statutory 5–16 sector.

In this book I will review how the different forms of preschool provision have arisen in the UK. I will consider how women's roles in childcare, education and other work are changing and how women can bring about change themselves. However, most women will not take up the challenges of change unless they are first of all assured that their children are emotionally secure, experiencing the best provision that can be offered, and unless they feel that as parents they are partners in their children's education and care. For these reasons, I explore here the issues of attachment, continuity in children's experiences, equal opportunities, the early years' curriculum, assessment of children's progress, staff and parental roles, and the UK's preschool provision compared to that in other countries.

A country that is trying to raise educational standards cannot afford to lose out by allowing its youngest children to be under-educated at a time in their development when they may be most open to new learning. But what do we mean by education for under-fives, what form should it take, what methods should be employed, and what role do adults need to adopt? As we also need care facilities to free parents to work, the most appropriate idea might be an *educare* system, offering high-quality care *and* education, and in this book I explore this possibility.

2
Under five in Britain

Recent calls for higher levels of preschool provision stem from two areas of need. The first relates to the benefits which parents believe their children will derive from being in a group with other children. This is additionally fuelled by the evidence gathered from research projects carried out since the late 1960s, both in Europe and the USA, indicating the long-term gains derived by children from such provision, especially where that provision aims to be educational. An increasing number of parents, from all socioeconomic backgrounds, seek such experiences for their young children. The second need for provision arises from the continued employment of mothers of children under five, either through economic necessity or the wish to remain in careers. In some cases, children living with a single father will also fall into this category of need.

The inadequacy and variability of preschool provision in the UK is well documented (see, for example, Blackstone, 1971; Pugh, 1988; Cohen, 1988; Moss, 1988) and it is highlighted by the trend for the voluntary organizations to take up the role of advocate, pointing out the inadequacy of funding for the under-fives, which they are well aware of due to their usual role as providers of services plugging the gaps. The Policy Analysis Unit Report (NCVO, 1986, p. 2) states:

> In Britain there is hardly any provision at all for two years olds and part-time care only for 20 per cent of three year olds. Low priority has been given by successive Governments to child-care for under-fives, and there is no longer any statutory responsibility on local authorities to provide facilities for preschool children, except those 'at risk'... So serious is the situation that in some areas

voluntary organisations now provide the only facilities available to parents of young children.

This statement was made in the same year as that which saw an outcry at the use of statistics by government statisticians who claimed that 88 per cent of the UK's three- and four-year-olds were in some form of educational or daycare provision (DES, 1986) placing the UK third in the European Community league table for preschool provision. By emphasizing provision to children aged over three, the difficulties for parents of under-threes and those needing full day care were masked.

In fact, the statistics collected by Pugh (1988) and Moss (1988) indicate that only 2 per cent of the under-twos are in publicly funded provision, while under one in ten of them attends a playgroup and the largest cohort of those whose parents need daycare are to be found in some of the 138,832 places provided by childminders in England, Scotland and Wales (combined). The 88 per cent quoted by DES (1986) derives from the provision for three- and four-year-olds, with 44 per cent in publicly funded services of whom 19 per cent are in the mainly part-time nursery school and nursery class provision; 20 per cent in the reception classes of primary schools, most of them attending for over six hours per day; 1 per cent in day nurseries or nursery centres; the rest of the 88 per cent is made up of the 40 to 45 per cent of three- and four-year-olds in playgroups, usually for an average of five or six hours per week; a further 1 per cent are among the growing population of under-fives attending private schools. The fact that the school entry age in the UK is lower than that in other EC countries also means that 100 per cent of five-year-olds are in school, thus producing an overall figure of attendance for children under six (school entry age in most of the other EC states) which compares quite favourably with other member nations. By the school year 1988–9 over 75 per cent of four-year-olds were attending primary schools (this includes nursery schools), the majority in reception classes.

In contrast to the government's claim, Moss (1988) places the UK near the bottom of the 'league table' for services for under-fives, owing to the fact that on closer analysis the availability of places for children under school age in the UK shows many weaknesses, for example the patchiness and variability in provision. The lack of co-ordination across the country and between services exacerbates the situation for individual families. Pugh (1988) found that many local authorities (in Great Britain) were attempting to develop a more coherent approach and working to break down the barriers between types of service. She emphasizes the need for consideration of the issues at national level, including discussion of the European Commission's proposal that parents be given extended leave during the first two years of a child's life. She adds that the UK was the only country to vote against this directive.

Co-ordination, also called for by the House of Commons Select Committee (1986; 1989), will hopefully produce a better overall service but it cannot do so in areas where there is no provision, or where the forms of provision are limited, particularly where the provision offered is fee-paying or part-time only. Similarly, greater awareness of the curricular needs of children under five must be a focus for discussion, whether provision in an area claims to be educational or not. Despite the fears of those who believe that to discuss ideas like curriculum will drive the spontaneity out of life in early childhood, we must realize that, willy-nilly, whether a child is at home, with a minder, in a nursery class, nursery centre or playgroup, he or she is learning. In other words, although in many instances no one would expect a written record of planned and spontaneous activities (in the home, for example), a curriculum is being offered and we need to ask ourselves what and how our children are learning through that curriculum, both the overt and the hidden. This learning begins at birth; some might argue that even before birth the effects of the mother's health, level of stress, lifestyle and environmental conditions are laying down factors which will influence the child's later educational achievement.

Some of the implications of differing forms of provision

There are two broad categories of organized preschool provision for children, when not in the care of their own parent or a parent-substitute: one takes the form of group provision in a building which is not someone's home; the other, provision in the child's own home or that of the provider. I shall call the two forms *centre-based* and *family-based* provision.

Examining the types of service falling into the family-based category one would probably list: childminders; small home-based playgroups; some toy libraries; Homestart, Portage and home-visiting schemes; some small community nurseries and crèches; and nannies and au pairs. In the centre-based category one could place: nursery schools; combined nursery centres and nursery classes; reception classes; hall-playgroups; day nurseries; assessment centres; opportunity groups; crèches; work-place nurseries; private nurseries; drop-in and family centres; playbuses; parent-and-toddler clubs; and some of the larger toy libraries.

Excluding the more specialized types of provision, one is left with three main strands within each type of provision: one is for the purposes of 'rescuing' (Blackstone, 1971) children of 'inadequate' parents; one for children of parents who are employed outside the home; one for children's pleasure, education and socialization.

Family-based provision could be said to encompass provision for which parents pay (childminding, nannies and au pairs; home-based playgroups and community nurseries); and home-based support which is offered by the local authority (educational home-visiting and Homestart). The latter provision is offered only to those families deemed to be in need, either because the child has learning difficulties or because the parents have problems. The former, it could be argued, can be further subdivided into working-class and middle-class provision. Dual-career, middle-class parents are more and more likely than their working-class counterparts, to employ a qualified person to come into their own home, often on a daily basis rather than living in, so that their young children may remain in their own environment, with their own possessions and leading lives as close as possible to those they might lead with their own parents. Solomon (1987) describes the difficulties which can still arise due to lack of clarity in expectations for both adult parties. She also expresses her reservations about the devaluing of children by parents who expect the work done for a pittance, as well as the immorality of liberated career women replacing themselves with other women, rather than challenging the system which would otherwise operate to impede their continuation in their careers.

Working-class parents employing child-minders, or paying fees to a community nursery, are likely to be very grateful for the service, rather than demanding support for their children's minders.

The problem is that women who are juggling a job and family usually have little time or energy left to fight campaigns for improvements in either the level or quality of preschool provision. While some will manage to obtain satisfactory care for their children, they may still feel they would like those children to benefit from educational group experience, but accept, reluctantly, that their own employment or difficulties for their childminder preclude such attendance for part of the day. Perhaps the best one can hope for is that they and their partners will support the campaigns of others, and when in later life such parents are no longer in need of this provision, they remain sympathetic to colleagues who do!

Centre-based provision similarly falls into three groups: publicly funded nursery schools and classes; reception classes, nursery centres and day nurseries (fees for which are means-tested, so that some parents will pay nothing because of their economic situation); and services for which most parents will be paying fees, such as playgroups and private nurseries. Despite the PPA claim that many groups are now found in working-class areas, the playgroup movement caters by and large for middle-class families. The divide in publicly-funded provision is caused by the placement of children deemed to come from 'problem families' in the day nurseries, while other, mainly working-class, children attend nursery schools, since many such schools were opened in areas where high levels of female employment had traditionally existed (for example, in the textile industry in Manchester, in pottery manufacture in Stoke-on-Trent), or areas defined as EPAs following the Plowden Report's (CACE, 1967) recommendations for compensatory provision before school for certain young inner-city children.

It would appear that in both family-based and centre-based provision there are different categories of facilities, which could in fact not only result in the labelling of children, but also influence the short-term and long-term gains those children make as a result. Children provided with home-visitors and those attending day nurseries may be stigmatized due to the notion that only inadequate parents are allocated such scarce resources. For example, nearly a quarter of all children in day nurseries are from ethnic minority groups (Moss, 1988), which suggests that those operating the referral system may not understand differences in cultural aspects of family life and, further, that a higher percentage of minority-group children may be labelled as coming from inadequate families in comparison with other groups in society. Children placed with childminders, despite much praiseworthy work on the part of the NCMA and local organizers, are still likely to be seen as participating in poorer-quality provision than that offered by professional staff, partly because research showed childminding to be failing between a third and a half of children studied (Mayall and Petrie, 1977; Bryant et al., 1980), and partly because the minders' own conditions of service and remuneration do not portend a high-quality service. This is unfortunate in some cases where the minder is indeed 'in it for love, not the money'; in addition, since the research was carried out, local authority social service departments have attempted to improve the quality of care. Some areas have followed a similar pattern to that of France, encouraging the minders to spend as much time as possible with their charges at a play centre where they are supported by other minders and by professionals, all of whom can advise on any difficulties. The research mentioned earlier stressed the need for minders and parents to spend time communicating with each other, and this advice applies equally well to other settings and the quality of provider–parent interactions.

Children who have places in nursery schools and classes are apparently the envy of most, since Bone's (1977) survey of parents' wishes for their children identified LEA provision as most sought after. In Osborn and

Milbank's (1987) research it was found that children who had attended maintained nursery classes did not fare as well, in tests at ten years of age, as those who had, according to their parents, been to nursery schools and playgroups. In fact, in some of the tests, they differed little from children without any preschool group experience. The children who appeared to fare best had attended nursery schools and small home playgroups, and for the latter group this may reflect other aspects of the children's lives as well as the need for adult–child ratios to be low (O'Connor, 1975; Sylva *et al.*, 1980).

Since the research relied heavily on parental knowledge of which form of provision the children attended, there may be some errors in it. Osborn and Milbank (1987) recognize the flaws in their work, pointing out, for example, that the non-group attenders with whom all others were being compared were likely to come from families which had experienced some of the greatest stresses during the children's early years. The work of Shinman (1981), Brown *et al.* (1975) and Brown and Harris (1978) has shown that the stresses affecting the lives of many children whose parents shy away from preschool group involvement are often unrelenting and apparently unpredictable.

The fact that so many variables impinged upon the lives of the children in Osborn and Milbank's (1987) study made it difficult to draw any firm conclusions about the comparative efficacy of nursery schools and playgroups, but since the nursery schools cater for more disadvantaged children and since playgroup children often come from homes where educational activities are encouraged in ways similar to those the child will meet at school (King, 1978; Sharp and Green, 1975; Davie *et al.*, 1984), the nursery schools were judged by the authors to be performing well. The issue of parental involvement in the child's preschool experience and subsequent parental involvement and interest in later education is also covered, and appears to be a good indicator of future success. More recent research by Tizard *et al.* (1988) reinforces our knowledge of the way in which preschool experiences have an impact upon achievement during the primary years of schooling. Although Woodhead (1985) warned that generalization of research evidence from other countries is dangerous – since different economic, ideological and other conditions will apply – long-term study of children in the USA whose parents were encouraged to see themselves as part of an educationally empowering system provides optimistic support for preschool provision of this type (Berruetta-Clement *et al.*, 1984).

The ecology of preschool provision

Bronfenbrenner's (1977; 1979) concentric circle model of the ecology of human development is a useful device for analysing the influences being brought to bear on the life of the young child. The innermost circle represents the *micro-system*, the individual's most immediate setting. Enclosing this is the *meso-system*, other settings and relationships which impinge on the child's experiences, for example, provision attended, the ways in which communication between the adults involved and the parents operates, and whether the child experiences continuity of experience or discontinuities, due to either changes in provider or differences in philosophy and culture between parent and teacher or minder. Many studies (for example, Cleave *et al*., 1982; Powell, 1980) indicate that most children experience discontinuity and fragmentation at the interface between family and provision. Bronfenbrenner's next layer, the *exo-system*, is made up of those structures which impinge less directly upon the children's lives but influence them through their parents, for example, parental employment, or the availability of a local authority committed to the provision of preschool facilities. The outer circle represents the *macro-system*, the overarching ideology and organization existing in the culture or subculture in which the child is growing up. This would include beliefs about the position of women and children in society, attitudes to single-parenthood, maternal employment, and so on.

Such a model can be used to analyse some of the possible experiences of our children. It can be used to establish whether the UK is committed to children, especially those coming from already disadvantaged homes and to equal rights for women. How can women take up equal roles in a society which does not help them with good provision for their children, so that they can feel confident in leaving them?

Four-year-olds in primary school

One group which was not considered in the above discussion comprises the children under five who are attending educational provision in reception classes in primary schools. The policy of a single September entry, whereby the child is admitted to school at the beginning of the academic year in which he or she reaches age five, has been common in some local authorities for many years, and has increased during the mid 1980s. This is, however, a contentious issue for several reasons. The fall in the birthrate and subsequent falling school rolls mean that schools have space to take extra children. Since there have been constant cries for more nursery provision, and parental awareness that summer-born children are still behind their classmates in some measures of attainment at age seven, it might appear that LEAs adopting this strategy were satisfying their customers by offering educational provision and at the same time ensuring that all children in a year–group experienced the same amount of schooling, in infant classes, before assessment or transfer at age seven. There are, however, various problems with this practice. First, achievement at seven is more likely to be related to the quality of the child's experiences during the early years than to the quantity of schooling. The study by Osborn and Millbank (1987) indicates that children under five generally derive greater benefits from nursery than from reception class attendance.

Barrett's (1986) evaluation of starting school raises the issue of the needs of the individual child entering the reception class. Her recommendations include the importance of teacher involvement in all areas of the curriculum, not just the 'basics', the fostering of self-direction in the children, space, time and adult support. The HMI survey of primary schools (DES, 1978a) highlighted the way in which older school children, whose day in class focused too narrowly upon the 'basics', performed less well in tests of reading and number work than did those pupils taught through a richer and more exciting curriculum. It seems possible that the younger the child, the greater the need for activities which, while developing the children's understanding of print, number, space, time, measurement and shape, also engage them in explorations and discoveries about materials, language, roles, relation-ships, symbolization through the use of words and fantasy play, and so on. In order to do this successfully, one teacher with a class of perhaps thirty young children, with no extra classroom assistance, will need to be 'Superteacher' and the children, while no doubt relying upon each other for assistance and support, will not have the opportunities for extending their language learning or discussions intended to provoke problem-solving. Their ability to enable their peers will be limited in comparison with that of a sensitive adult. Further arguments about the inadvisability of such provision relate to the 'knock-on effect' in the nurseries and play-groups, where the advantageous mix of older children with those aged three and under is lost and each year there is a mass exodus of children, rather than small groups moving in and out over the whole year.

The difficulties faced by those children now in reception classes at four have been detailed by Bennett (1987), Sharp (1987), Sestini (1987), Stevenson (1987), and by Bennett and Kell (1989). Statements issued by the BAECE and the PPA (1987) and the NAPE (1986) have called for such classes to receive staffing, resourcing and facilities equivalent to those of good nursery provision. The NAHT (1987) also added its voice to this call for appropriate provision for three- and four-year-olds. Many of the teachers involved in teaching four-year-olds in reception classes have felt inadequately trained and plead for in-service courses, particularly where they need to be able to articulate to parents the importance of learning through play, part-time attendance related to the needs of the individual child and record-keeping and assessment of children in this setting.

Sadly, one wonders why some of these groups were not so concerned about conditions in reception classes when the average age of the pupils was a few months older. Perhaps the four-year-olds will have done a favour for those children who, at five (or 'rising' five) found the primary school a harsh, serious and alien environment. What we should all consider is the way in which we can, as a society, provide for each child what he or she needs in terms of early educational experiences and how we can develop a policy so that parents who work may *choose* to work in more flexible ways during their child's early years, so that neither parents nor children suffer. One of the salient features of the research by Bennett and Kell (1989) is the finding that tasks set for children by reception class teachers are poorly matched to their abilities. Classes based on a nursery, rather than on a junior school, tradition will not operate in this way. Children will be free for the most part to choose, initiate and develop their own tasks, with the adults acting as facilitators. In this way tasks are much more likely to be well matched to children's abilities. Early in the twentieth century Margaret McMillan (1930) suggested that we needed nursery schools for children aged three to eight, for this was the style of provision which she advocated for the early years and not the practice of top-down junior methods imposed on the teachers and children of an infant department. The demise of the majority of separate infant or first schools, for economic reasons, may be in part responsible for the resulting ethos in some early years classrooms, one which is inappropriate for our youngest children.

CONTEXTS AND CONSTRAINTS

3
Histories: a tale of two Departments

A great deal of the criticism aimed at the current state of under-fives provision focuses on the difficulties which arise as a result of administration by two different government departments – the Department of Education and Science (DES) and the Department of Health and Social Security (DHSS).* What does this imply, then, for the children under five whose experiences are being supervised by workers from different backgrounds, in terms of training, expectations, experiences and attitudes?

In order to reflect on these differences, we must first ask how the situation came about. Why have we in the UK inherited a system where the dichotomy between provision designated as care and that recognized as education is, at one and the same time, more clearly divided yet more complex than that in other European countries? I begin by examining the history of early childhood provision outside the home.

Scarr and Dunn (1987) claim that when women were needed to work in the fields, or in trades, before the Industrial Revolution, society was in no hurry to stress their children's need for constant attention. Of course, we might argue that the small children would be cared for by another member of the household, or would accompany the mother, soon to be engaged in an aspect of the parent's occupation, so that separation of mother and child was not an issue until work of the type initiated by the Industrial Revolution made the lot of mother and accompanying infant too difficult. However, Scarr and Dunn (1987) add that it was this change in society which altered the expectations placed upon women. The cult of domesticity and motherhood was to keep women 'in their place' and one sees this romantic view of women reflected in paintings of the time:

*The DHSS became two departments at the end of 1988.

middle-class women are portrayed as 'angels' ministering to men who must face the harsh realities of life out in the world of machinery, amid the growing animosity of a hungry, underfed and overworked labour force, with frequent 'trouble at t'mill'. Working-class mothers became increasingly regarded as either inadequate or uncaring, because of their inability to compare favourably with their middle-class counterparts. For the latter, too, the job of parenting was in any case becoming more complex; love alone was not enough. By the end of the nineteenth century there was an upsurge in the provision of training colleges for nannies. Thus the emphasis for better-off families and their children was on the development of the whole child. In contrast, the discovery of physical weaknesses in the conscripts called to fight during the First World War, due to poor diet and lack of treatment for illnesses during early childhood, caused philanthropists to focus on the physical needs of children of the poor. These two strands, with the influence of German immigrant textile workers importing Froebelian principles into the middle-class kindergarten, and the dual purposes of humanitarian rescue and social control inducing the acceptance of three- and four-year-olds in elementary schools, underlie our situation to this day.

A few philanthropists attempted to provide similar experiences for 'slum' children to those experienced by children from more affluent families. Robert Owen believed that the children of the workers in his New Lanarkshire factory should be provided for in ways which would find echoes in today's nurseries, with painting, dancing, singing and without the kind of rote learning of reading which would later form the main school curriculum. Owen believed that environmental factors, particularly during the earliest years of life, shaped the future citizen, and what he worked for was the education of an engaged future citizenry, not a subjugated or underachieving one. Although Owen was active in this way over 150 years ago, his example, like those of other outstanding pioneers, shames our so-called progress as a civilized society. Soon after the 1870 Education Act, the elementary schools which provided almost exclusively for children of poor labouring classes, became part of the compulsory national education system. Around the same time, William Mather, in Manchester, began two philanthropic kindergartens, but these were so popular that the staff were probably unable to operate under the type of conditions Froebel would have advocated. Blackstone (1971) details the other types of establishment, the charity, dame, industry and common day-schools which were prepared to offer places to children under five. She describes the way in which the demands for child labour in the UK were probably a highly influential factor in the slow development of schooling, in comparison with other European countries.

It was certainly the reason why the formal age of entry to school in the UK is five, while it is six or seven on the Continent, for it was argued that if children must attend school, the sooner it was over and they were free to enter the workforce the better. By the turn of the century, 43 per cent of the country's three-, four- and five-year-olds were attending Board schools, or private kindergartens and infant schools. The classes were often very large, sixty pupils to one teacher, none of whom had nursery training, since such no training existed at that time. Reading the sensitive reports of Katherine Bathurst, one of the women inspectors to the Board of Education, one can understand their recommendation that children under five should not be taught in elementary schools, but in nursery schools.

> Let us now follow the baby of three years through part of one day of school life. He is placed on a hard wooden seat (sometimes it is only the step of a gallery) . . . He often cannot reach the floor with his feet and in many cases he has no back to lean against. He is told to fold his arms and sit quiet . . . The difficulty of breathing in this constrained position is considerable, but he hunches his shoulders bravely to make his arms longer . . . At a given signal every child in the class begins calling out mysterious sounds . . . I have actually heard one baby class repeat one sound a hundred and twenty times continuously . . . (Bathurst, 1905, p. 121).

Sadly, the words of these inspectors were heeded only in part. Children under five were officially excluded from elementary schools but no nursery schools were provided. Despite the pioneering work of Margaret and Rachel McMillan, little was achieved before the First World War, and the latter itself halted further action. Although the 1918 Education Act allowed LEAs to allocate funds for pre-primary provision, only 15.3 per cent of under-fives were attending any form of maintained school.

The time between the wars was one in which there was a reiteration of the ideology of motherhood, home as the best place for the preschool child, except in cases where, once again, provision was deemed necessary as rescue from an inadequate or working mother, or impoverished circumstances. This message was enshrined in the Hadow Report (Consultative Committee, 1933) on infant and nursery schools, despite the presence on the Committee of Susan Isaacs, who was already renowned for her important work on children's early education and who, in her work at London University, set up the first Department of Child Development, which has influenced so many of the later disseminators of good nursery practice. Much of Isaacs's writing is as relevant today as it was when published. She stressed (Isaacs, 1954) the need for early experiences to be educational in a holistic way, stating her belief that school has two main functions: to provide for the child's own bodily and social skills and means of expression; and, like Bruner's spiral curriculum, to 'open' the facts of the real world. For Isaacs, this real world was not school subjects but cross-curricular activities, having meaning and relevance for the children, activities and ideas which would arouse and capitalize upon their curiosity, to touch, take apart, ask questions, at this vital stage in life.

Again, as with Owen and the McMillan sisters, it is difficult to understand why successive UK governments have failed to grasp the implications of the importance of the early years and the need for quality experiences for all the population during this time in each individual's life, with such rational and persuasive influences attempting to draw attention to these ideas.

However, they have not and it was still with rescue in mind that by 1938 there were 118 nursery schools and 104 day nurseries. With the outbreak of the Second World War, mothers of young children were required to help with the war effort by taking employment in various essential industries. They also needed to supplement the low pay of their husbands in the armed forces. Thus it was as a result of the need for daycare for all under-fives, and for working hours, that the Ministry of Health was given the main task of setting up wartime nurseries. The then Ministry of Labour was asked to co-ordinate the work of the Ministries of Education and Health in this respect, because of the need for siting nursery provision in the areas where women's labour would be required. Even allowing for the fact that human beings tend to behave in apparently illogical ways when under stress, and war cannot be regarded otherwise, it probably seems strange to us, retrospectively, that a country so keen to enforce the role of women as full-time mothers, as witnessed in the Hadow Report (Consultative Committee, 1933) and reiterated later in the Plowden Report (CACE, 1967), should decide not only that children could do without their mothers in the interests of the nation, but also that some of them could be evacuated to live with unfamiliar families, who often had little experience of under-fives. Of course, to be fair, it was the children's physical safety which was at the forefront of society's thoughts when nursery schools in potential bombing target areas were closed because they did not have air-raid shelters and the children in those parts of the country were sent away from their own families to more rural locations.

The scale of the increase in other preschool provision during the war years, to relieve pressures on working families, was not, however, extensive. Nevertheless, attitudes towards nursery education and women's employment were thought to be influenced by experiences forced upon the population during these years. A committee, chaired by R.H. Tawney, known as the Council for Educational Advance, and representing the NUT, the TUC, the WEA and the Co-operative Union Education Committee, advocated nursery education as part of a list of high-priority reforms, which it urged as essential to the achievement of equality of opportunity. Even *The Times*, in its editorial of 19 July 1942, supported the ideal of 'full and proper provision for the preschool child'. The 1943 White Paper (Board of Education, 1943) which preceded the 1944 Education Act was the first official statement to give any recognition to the value of nursery school attendance to all children. It acknowledged that such schools were needed in all areas, since even children who come from 'good' homes could derive much educational and physical benefit from them.

Although some of the day nursery provision was transferred to the Ministry of Education after the war, with a consequent cut in hours and days of provision, the two ministries failed to co-ordinate their efforts and, more importantly, the Ministry of Education failed to ensure the implementation of the requirements of the 1944 Education Act, which had placed the duty to provide nursery education in the hands of LEAs. For the next twenty years, nursery provision was to be the victim of financial restrictions. The limited resources available for education were channelled into the statutory sector, where numbers had risen as a result of the post-war 'baby boom'. Official Circulars during this period constantly issued statements of regret. No government since 1944 had been able to undertake preschool expansion, until in 1964 an addendum to Circular 8/60 allowed restrictions to be lifted so that nursery places could be offered to the children of women teachers, so desperate was the shortage of qualified personnel in schools at that time. It seems bizarre that a generation later we are again experiencing this apparent inability on the part of government to plan effectively.

When the Plowden Report (CACE, 1967) called for the inception of educational priority areas in which nursery education was to play a central role, it called also for such provision, part-time for all children over three years of age, on demand. The DES (1972) White Paper, presented by Margaret Thatcher as the then Secretary of State for Education, reacted positively to the Plowden Committee's recommendations, proposing that by 1980 there would be places in nursery schools and classes for 50 per cent of three-year-olds and 90 per cent of four-year-olds.

The economic recession dashed any hopes that such plans would be fulfilled. The 1980 Education Act altered the *obligation* placed upon LEAs by the 1944 Act, to provide nursery education, reducing this to a *power*, in other words, such provision was at the discretion of the LEA and its existence would therefore depend on the philosophy and financial position of local councils, as well as the ability of local groups to exercise pressure upon them to recognize the need for priority spending in this sector.

There may be many and varied reasons for the well nigh exponential development of playgroup provision during the years since Belle Tutaev's letter to the *Guardian* in 1961 which started the playgroup movement. It was – and, some would argue, still is – a largely middle-class movement, and those who were first involved were young well-educated mothers who found themselves in homes remote from their extended families, due to the new professional mobility required of their executive husbands. Partly as a result of lack of maintained provision and extremely poor childminding arrangements, and partly of post-war propaganda ensuring that they would believe that their children would fare best if they gave up their careers on the birth of their first child, such women often found themselves in unfamiliar towns, villages or cities, with two small children (on average), and few places where they were welcome other than the park or the occasional development by a benign Mothers' Union. They were keen to help their offspring to a good start and were eager to pursue various activities with them at home, but they also realized that both the children and they themselves needed the company of their peers. At the time, the movement was to be a stopgap provision for the children, part of the pressure group of the National Campaign for Nursery Education. It was only when the 1972 White Paper threatened nursery expansion which would doubtless have ended with the closure of many playgroups that members of the PPA rallied in their own defence and against such moves. Their reasons were based upon the experiences of the movement during the previous decade, in which they had come to understand that through parental involvement, initially the playgroups' way of keeping down costs, they had stumbled upon the vital and exciting ingredient which made their groups different from nursery schools and classes. This involvement, they claimed, was important in that it not only affected the life of the local community, but also meant that the children, whose mothers (and sometimes fathers) became involved in day-to-day activities, gained both directly and indirectly, because these parents took home the educative practices of the play sessions, as well as developing their own adult skills and confidence. By 1975 playgroups catered for almost a quarter of the three- and four-year-olds in England and Wales (Pugh, 1988), while only just over one in ten of this age group attended maintained nursery provision. During the life of the playgroup movement, its officers have worked enthusiastically to acquire grant aid for groups, for the employment of advisers, for courses at a variety of levels, and to provide some expenses for the voluntary area organizers, who co-ordinate networks of groups. Many playgroup branches also fostered the development of parent-and-toddler clubs to cater for those with children too tiny to attend a playgroup. The total membership of this powerful, democratic organization is around 14,000 groups, but due to the imbalance of local authority provision, centring on the urban areas, and the greater difficulties experienced in setting up playgroups in less privileged neighbourhoods, the movement each year shows an overall ratio of 40:60, urban to rural, groups for England and Wales as a whole (PPA, 1986). Despite severe financial problems, which came to a head in criminal proceedings against one employee in 1985, the organization continues to take on extra responsibilities, such as 'drop-in groups', DHSS 'Opportunities for Volunteering', hospital groups, and other initiatives involving under-fives and their families, because there is no other body under whose wing these groups can find support.

The demographic changes which will result in a crisis shortage of workers in the 1990s have resulted in the playgroup movement's leaders negotiating with government and employers for a major involvement in any expansion of daycare facilities. Cynics might suggest that this is welcomed because playgroups, with the vast involvement of volunteers, will cost considerably less to operate than a proper nursery or daycare system. Why has the organization which claimed in the early 1970s, when supposedly under attack from planned nursery expansion, that its main strength is its parental participation, become embroiled in this way?

The PPA is an important pressure group when issues relating to early childhood are raised in Parliament, particularly in evidence to Select Committees. It joined with the BAECE in a statement expressing concern for the four-year-olds who are increasingly entering reception classes, but without facilities equivalent to those in nursery provision (BAECE and PPA, 1987). We can only assume the policy of involvement in negotiations about workplace crèches and the like, is in order to ensure that a voice for parents is heard.

The history of childminders, and also of day nurseries, illustrates the way in which the development of preschool provision in this country has been a reactive rather than proactive process. Like the educational reports already mentioned, statements issued by the Ministries of Health and Education (1945) argued that

under normal peace-time conditions the right policy to pursue would be positively to discourage mothers of children under two from going out to work, to make provision for children between two and five by way of nursery schools and nursery classes; and to regard day nurseries and day guardians as supplements to meet special needs.

Local authorities, as stated above, are now only 'empowered' to provide day nurseries, for which charges may be made to parents, although in practice this may amount to a small contribution following a means test. Furthermore, the gathering together under the DHSS umbrella of day nurseries, private nurseries, childminders and playgroups, subject to the 1980 Child Care Act and the 1948 Nurseries and Childminders Regulation Act, means that the majority of children under five, unless they are fortunate in local initiatives to link with education, will be missing out on valuable experiences which may affect their later educational achievement. Amendments to the 1989 Children's Act were put forward to remedy some of the shortcomings, but, according to Pugh (1987), few local authorities offer the kind of support to childminders which is really necessary, and which was highlighted by research (see, for example, Bryant *et al.*, 1980). Warwickshire is one area where the networking and support to childminders is of a high standard, achieved by the enthusiasm and commitment of key workers, but, as with other parts of the country, funds for training all under-fives workers are woefully inadequate. This means there are grave difficulties when multi-professional courses are initiated to foster co-operation.

The House of Commons Select Committee (1986; 1989) Reports have recommended the co-ordination of existing facilities for under-fives, with this responsiblity being delegated to LEAs. Bradley (1982) reported that, following his national survey, many of the challenges thrown up by attempts at co-ordination resulted from territorial behaviour on the part of some of those involved, sometimes at grassroots level, often at managerial levels in local administration. For example, social services depend heavily upon playgroups in many areas, and were the myriad volunteers to down tools (as well they might if the shortage of workers in other sectors makes life in preschool provision less and less attractive financially compared with other employment) not only would the lives of social workers be made more difficult, but also the view of community life from a social worker's perspective would be diminished. On the other hand, social services support for playgroups can be perceived as a threat by education department workers who view the service provided by nursery schools and classes as superior to what playgroups can offer children in a makeshift environment, with untrained workers (by education standards), and with limited equipment and sporadic (for the individual child) sessions.

Bradley (1982) suggests ways of overcoming many of the difficulties, and Tomlinson (1986) describes such an initiative in Cheshire. The work in nursery centres (Ferri *et al.*, 1981) and in Strathclyde, where the co-ordination of all services for preschool children is already operational, is likely to be the focus of much debate and further research, if co-ordination is to become a reality. The Strathclyde initiative includes giving power over funding of some £20 million to the pre-fives committee which co-ordinates work of education and social service employees. This type of delegation of power has been seen as a crucial element in the potential success of any joint ventures (see Bruner, 1980), since committees with no executive powers, cutting across departmental boundaries, will have no 'teeth' if they are unable to offer material benefit or incentives to already overstretched staffs. A second element which bodes well for the Strathclyde venture is the importance attached to community involvement, although some members of their committee feel that too much bureaucracy may still impede the engagement of some of the more reluctant parents, alienated due to their own painful experiences as children in contacts with local department professionals. Here again there is also some evidence of antagonism between play-groups and the Education Department, in part exacerbated by the claim that playgroups function only in more affluent areas. In Strathclyde there are a number of Scottish PPA developments, funded through Urban Aid, and the local chairperson (Thorburn, 1987) feels that these illustrate the way in which playgroups can be more flexible, having a broader brief than that of nursery education. What is essential in any analysis of the effects of divisions in under-fives provision is the reflection upon the possible experiences of any individual child, and the way in which that child's preschool needs may be different from another's. In fact, some needs are simply not being met by a system which is so patchy and unco-ordinated (Pugh, 1988): in particular, it does not always offer continuity of experience by linking with primary schools; and, as we shall see later, it does not always offer the best possible educational environment for a child during the years of optimal learning opportunity, or for setting the pattern of learning how to learn.

4
Psychologies: attachment versus attendance

It has been argued that the lack of any policy aiming at preschool provision for all under-fives whose parents so wished has been due to a deeply-held British belief in the importance of the family, and especially the biological mother, for the young child. This belief is said to have fostered the post-war adoption of the conclusions of Bowlby's (1951) early research on the damaging influence of mother–child separation. It is also said to explain the closure of many of the nurseries which the Ministry of Health had 'sold' during the Second World War as educationally and socially good for children (Scarr and Dunn, 1987), though Riley (1983) argues that the closure of the war nurseries had much more to do with arguments between government departments over finance and a wish to transfer costs to local authorities than with state anxiety about the effects of maternal deprivation upon the next generation.

More recently, Mullan (1987) has concurred with Riley in suggesting that it is naive of writers, such as Graham (1985), to suggest that ideas and research 'findings' could have had such a profound influence upon policy – perhaps the boot of naivety is rather on the other foot and the feminist writers Mullan chastises are perfectly aware that Bowlby's work was being used as emotional propaganda, inducing guilt and anxiety in order to evade the issue of continued preschool provision and women in the workforce in what, before the war, had been traditionally male occupations. As further example of the contradictions in attitudes to motherhood and employment, contrast the fact that nursery places were to be provided for teachers who were the mothers of young children, to enable them to return to work at a time when there was a shortage of teachers, (DES, 1964) with the statement of the Plowden Committee (CACE, 1967, para. 330), deploring

> the increasing tendency of mothers of young children to work . . . it is generally undesirable, except to prevent a greater evil, to separate mother and child for a whole day in a nursery . . . it is no business of education service to encourage these mothers.

Clearly, we need to examine the issues involved, investigating the claims of those who believe the whole effort to push women back into the home with their young children occurred as a reaction to women's growing autonomy – and what could be more effective than to attack women by implying that they damage their children by their own actions? A further outcome of this 'no-policy policy' has been a division in the ranks of women themselves. On the one hand, those who wish to stay at home with their children, and can afford to do so, feel vulnerable because they are sensitive to pressures exhorting them to liberate themselves from the role of housewife (labelled 'low-status'). On the other hand, those who wish to (or have to) carry on working, feel that they are perceived as heartless and uncaring towards their family, while at the same time being vulnerable to the charge that they will be less efficient because of family commitments. This division bears testimony to the strange way in which our society prefers to categorize women, with a dichotomy between woman as worker and woman as mother, while for men this duality of roles is not a problem. It has been suggested that the war effort was 'special', that women were glad to return to their homes and children (Riley, 1983), and that to have done otherwise would have involved women in a new 'war', one in which they would have been fighting to be taken seriously as workers.

In all the tangle concerning women and employment, the first question we must ask is, irrespective of whether children would otherwise be at home with their mothers, whether they are damaged by or benefit from preschool provision outside the home. It is only after examining the evidence relating to children that we can move on to consider the rights and roles of the adults involved.

Paving the way for John Bowlby

The Industrial Revolution brought in its wake a view of womanhood, or at least of middle-class womanhood, which was to influence subsequent generations of British girls and women. For working-class women the outlook was bleak. Where in earlier times they had worked hard at home or in the fields, many now found themselves almost invisible – faceless, quiet, subservient, as domestic servants; or faceless as part of the masses working in the new industries, leaving their offspring to fend for themselves until they, too, could join the labour force; or faceless as the victims of Victorian values, choosing between the workhouse and prostitution. Since most of the work carried out by women at this time was demeaning in one way or another, is it surprising that, for middle-class women, home and family were to become their occupation? They were to be household managers. Furthermore, the romanticism of the mid-nineteenth century was to initiate a view of the child in which mother-love was central and child rearing a complex task (Scarr and Dunn, 1987). A simplistic attitude towards the growing awareness of the poor state of health among army recruits around the turn of the century, later the cause of the provision of school meals, focused attention on the need for mothers to be taught to look after future citizens (and soldiers?) properly.

In the United States and the UK now-famous men gained recognition as the experts on children and childcare – from John Watson, Arnold Gesell, Sigmund Freud, Herbert Spencer and G. Stanley Hall, to Truby King, D.W. Winnicott, and Dr Benjamin Spock. During the first half of the twentieth century there was gradual acceptance that girls should be educated, but even as late as 1963 the Newsom Report (DES, 1963) reiterated the earlier view that the education of girls should prepare them for their expected future roles as wives and mothers. For many women, careers ended with marriage. The educability of children was seen as dependent upon the work already carried out at home by the mother. Winnicott's radio broadcasts in 1944 carried the clear message 'do not leave your children and go out to work'. It is tempting to surmise that the educability in question was preparedness for literacy. However, as far as most teachers were concerned, parental instruction in early reading, at home, was taboo. Initiation into literacy, and presumably numeracy, was clearly regarded as the role of the school. So what was it that caused the insistence upon the intimate and crucial nature of the mother–child relationship?

Attachment and bonding

The concept of attachment describes the powerful emotional tie a young baby feels in relation to its caretaker – usually its mother. The animal ethologist Konrad Lorenz used the idea to explain the behaviour of goslings following the first moving object they see on hatching, or lambs following farm children when a ewe dies: they become attached to mother substitutes. Thus the idea that the mother who gave birth to a child must be the object of the baby's attachment became prevalent and the further concept – bonding – was posited as occurring in the mother due to instinct and hormones. As far as children are concerned,

> Attachment is the tendency for the child to show a marked preference for a particular person, to want to be near her, especially when frightened, tired or ill, and to protest if she goes out of sight. Attachment behaviour becomes less intense after about the age of three, but remains important until at least the age of six years (Tizard, 1986, p. 4).

Bowlby (1953; 1969) argued that all children are biologically programmed to form this attachment to their principal caretaker, remaining attached through thick and thin, and that children who are subjected to variable or abusive treatment will, later in life, bear the scars, in the form of an inability to form lasting and meaningful relationships. Furthermore, any new relationships made during childhood will be doomed to replicate the first, at least from the child's perspective. Ainsworth *et al.* (1974), Bowlby's colleagues, developed this work further, carrying out experimental work with children aged one to two years, in which the children's mothers were asked to bring them into a strange room, leave them in the room with a stranger and then rejoin them, each child being observed alone in this situation. Children who use their mothers as a base, who are disturbed by her departure but comforted by her return, greeting her warmly, and who show a preference for her over the stranger are said to be *securely attached*. Children not displaying such behaviour, for example, those who explore freely whether or not the mother is present, or those who show no anger or distress, are said to be *insecurely attached*. Ainsworth *et al.* (1974) suggest that the insecurely attached children (about one-third in US research) had experienced maternal deprivation through their mothers' inadequate sensitivity, despite their constant presence, rather than as a result of being left with others. Through longitudinal research, Ainsworth *et al.* (1974) conclude that children who are securely attached at one year were the recipients, during the first year of life, of more physical and eye contact, more affection and soothing than the insecure infants, and that the secure one-year-olds, subsequently became competent three- to six-year-olds, showing greater independence, self-esteem and social competence at nursery school.

It is important to remember that Bowlby's early work was based upon studies of children who had been subjected to residential institutional care at the hands of grossly overstretched staff, most of whom would have perceived the most essential aspects of their work as health and hygiene. Furthermore, evidence from studies of primates (for example, Harlow, 1961) was often cited to indicate the terrible consequences of maternal deprivation. Whatever we may feel about the applicability of primate studies, even those more relevantly conducted in natural surroundings, the view that it is normal for a primate mother to be sole caretaker of her offspring is not borne out, and one can counter such an argument by stating that were we to live in a natural way we might indeed find that the mother became the initial carer but that she would be supported by, and share the care of offspring with, other members of the group. A further argument used is to stress the role of the mother in history, yet if one examines the situation one will probably find that many children did have other carers because their mothers died in subsequent child births, or their mothers had so many children that they had little time for any but the latest additions to their brood. Despite criticisms of his work and of the flimsiness of supposedly supporting evidence by others, we must acknowledge a great debt to Bowlby in that his work, and that of his followers, drew attention to the sad plight of children in residential care and children in hospital, but an unfortunate characteristic of the popularization of a theory is that it is adopted inflexibly and under inappropriate conditions. Support for the concept of mother–infant bonding was also seized upon through Freudian theory – that the child's attachment behaviour, intended to maintain the proximity of the bonded adult, was due to the child's pleasure-seeking. Such theorizing produced even greater pressure on parents, or rather mothers, to feel guilty if they deprived their small children of their presence. Thus, with Bowlby's blessing, mothers were discouraged from using alternative carers, even relatives, for children under three, and only brief, part-time separation was believed to be appropriate for preschool children over this age.

Later research evidence countering Bowlby's ideas can be fully examined in Rutter (1981). Tizard and Tizard (1983) support the finding that even institutionalized children in well-staffed and equipped residential homes, despite having no experience of mothering by one permanent adult, did not develop the affectionless characters Bowlby predicted, nor did all separations from a mother result in long-term effects. One of the main criticisms of all the theorizing by the men who had become the child-rearing gurus, is that they focused too narrowly on the mother–infant pair, forgetting not only the father and siblings, but members of the extended family, close friends and the context in which all these community members interacted. Research (for example Ainsworth, 1973; Maccoby and Jacklin, 1974; Schaffer, 1977; Yarrow, 1967) has shown that young children do not have a predisposition to form a unique and especially powerful bond with the mother, although their relationship with her may be one of several special to the child.

There is also evidence to suggest that from the first year of life children benefit from opportunities to form different social contacts. We know from our experience as adults that extending our network of friends does not dilute our feelings towards older friends, so why should a child experience any reduction in attachment to his or her mother on forming new bonds with others? What seems to be important about attachment is that the person to whom the child becomes attached is familiar, although that familiarity need not necessarily be due to the amount of contact time – kibbutz-reared children attach to their parents whom they see less than their *metapulet*, or nurse (Rabin, 1965). The degree of attachment seems to depend upon the adult's responsiveness to the child, the intensity and one-to-one nature of the interactions (Tizard, 1986). It is perhaps simplest to say that the child feels special to that person and detects the honesty in the other person's interest.

What are the special characteristics of attachment relationships?

In an attempt to clarify the particular aspects of attachment in older preschool children, Webb (1984) investigated the relationships of nineteen children aged four to six years. Although her study was conducted in the USA, it seems highly improbable that her results do not hold relevance for other Western societies. All the children lived with both parents (Webb felt that other factors would have impinged upon the results had she included one-parent families, divorced or separated parents, etc.), and both parents worked long hours outside the home. Thus the children spent roughly forty hours per week in some form of preschool group, or care provision, and often had only about another forty hours in waking contact time with their parents. Webb derived her evidence from observations, questionnaires and children's story sessions, and she found that the children were most closely attached to their parents, despite the long hours of group attendance, that they were also attached to other family members, siblings and grandparents, despite the often infrequent contact with the latter, and to a range of other contacts, such as teachers, teenage baby sitters, friends' parents and so on. One child had, during the first few years of life, experienced over twenty different carers, many of them daytime minders. In spite of this, he was judged to have special relationships with his parents, similar in quality to those of the other children in the group.

The features which made their relationships with their parents special were 'bugging and nudging'; use of pet names; and idiosyncratic behaviour. *Bugging and nudging* is typified by an adult's apparent nagging, direct or indirect, positive or negative – for example, asking the child to sing a song for grandma, or to eat up food because the parent wants a big strong child – which serves to demonstrate to the child that he or she is special and important. This type of behaviour is comparable to the 'goal-directed partnership stage' posited by Bowlby (1969), in that parent and child interact and the child has the possibility of influencing the sensitive adult's inputs, so that there is a good 'fit' between them. Such 'bugging and nudging', Webb suggests, are powerful indicators to the children that the adults in question have an 'investment' in them and the interaction becomes mutually gratifying. The use of *pet names*, and its concomitant (when showing disapproval), the use of the full given name, act as binding functions – again emphasizing the special, and sometimes private and intimate nature of the relationship. *Idiosyncratic behaviour* refers to shared rituals, favourite stories and other aspects peculiar to the parent–child pair, or to close family members.

Can fathers equal mothers in attachment?

Fathers were allowed only a rather back stage role in the theories of some of the mid-twentieth-century advisers. For example, Winnicott (1964) suggested that the father was involved through his relationship with the mother, who encircled the child in her own arms. For a variety of reasons, such rigid stereotypes have been challenged since the Second World War, and fathers have become much more involved in day-to-day activities with their children, as Newson and Newson (1965) documented, although some still appear to pick up the more enjoyable aspects of childcare and leave the more arduous tasks to their partners (Oakley, 1974; Clarke-Stewart, 1982; Webb, 1984).

Bonding between father and child, as one might expect, appears to depend on both length of exposure to each other and on the quality of such encounters (Jackson, 1984) and, while Lamb (1982) suggests that the quality of the relationships between each of two parents and their infant may differ, the importance of the father–child relationship is likely to depend upon the degree to which the father is involved in child rearing. Most importantly, Main and Weston's (1981) work indicates that children who are securely attached to both parents are the most sociable, children attached securely to mothers only are somewhat less sociable, and those attached to fathers only the least sociable by comparison. This would appear to be quite logical on the part of the child: if you already enjoy the company of more than one adult, you may feel more confident to try a third, but if you know only one well after a reasonable period of life, perhaps your ability to 'dance' with more than one partner is affected. This analogy with dance seems particularly apt. It is used by Stern (1977), who suggests that even missteps, after which we adjust (if we are sensitive), are important and exciting aspects of this dance of life.

Other partners children may have encountered before they meet a preschool worker could be siblings, au pairs, nannies and so on. Could they have bonded with any of these, and, if so, does this bode well or ill for the child entering the nursery or playgroup? As far as nannies and au pairs are concerned, one would expect that the length and quality of the interactions, as with fathers, would affect the existence of and intensity of bonding. Mullan (1987) dismisses this group as of little importance on the grounds that they impinge on the lives of a small, aristocratic percentage of the population. But as many professional women continue their careers after childbirth, and employ other younger women to work in their homes, this group is more likely to be an increasing than a dwindling one. Webb's (1984) study indicates that, while children do form attachments to these young caretakers, these attachments do not cause a diminution in intensity of the attachment to the parents, as Mead (1943) suggested they did in her study of children cared for in large homogeneous households in Samoa. Mead was in fact suggesting that this was advantageous to the children because they were less likely to suffer trauma in the event of loss of parents. Minuchin's (1974) 'enmeshed' and 'disengaged' family styles are useful classificatory devices for thinking about the ways in which some families encourage their children to befriend other caring adults. *Enmeshed* families prefer to enlist only close relatives to share child rearing, while *disengaged* families are more open to non-relatives. The enmeshed family is more likely to experience anxiety if, for example, grandma either works or lives too far away to free the parents. Similarly, an enmeshed family is more likely to be ambivalent towards hired help – and it is perhaps parental feelings and attitudes, transmitted to the child, which are the factors likely to cause damage to the child, not the actual change of carer. In the same way, the happier the parent feels and encourages the child to feel about group attendance, the more successful that attendance is likely to be.

In parallel with differences in family values, the differences in cultural values will be likely to affect the child's ability to form an attachment with a teacher or playgroup supervisor. Over a quarter of a century ago, Whiting (1963) pointed out that, in contrast to other cultures, white

American society, a society with similar views about motherhood to those held in other Western cultures, placed a far higher priority on the presence of the mother at home than did the other five cultures she studied. More recent studies (Clarke-Stewart *et al*., 1983) also comment on this feature and there is no evidence that daycare by someone who is not the child's mother causes any damage to the child, if the takeover is planned, gradual and positive for all concerned.

A further factor which appears to influence the ease or difficulty experienced by a child in developing attachments with other adults outside the home is that of the child's basic 'style'. Webb (1984) placed the children she studied in three main categories: the outgoing, social, verbal child; the shy, self-contained child; and the oppositional, persistent, sometimes aggressive child. The persistence of two of these styles in the home and the group for the children in her study indicates the great importance of communication between parent and worker and the need for a gentle transition from home to group life, with the parent present during early settling-in sessions. The children who were initially shy and self-contained in the group sessions could eventually move into either of the other two styles – the development of the most positive and, one would guess, for the child, happier, style might depend upon the sensitivity of the parent-educarer collaboration.

In the group setting, children have opportunities to form relationships with other children. Rubin (1980) concludes from his observations of three-year-olds, that they form quite sophisticated relationships with other children, including children met at playgroup or nursery. However, as Tizard (1986) points out, there has been little research into the ways in which children's relationships in one setting influence those developed in another. Rubenstein and Howes's (1983) work suggests that the widening of children's social networks to include peers has a beneficial effect in the sense that they become less dependent upon their mothers and develop greater autonomy. If children have formed strong attachments to parents and others during their early years, it seems they will not be damaged by group attendance as long as the provision is good-quality group provision. Tizard (1986) speculates from the research evidence available at present, that provision for children under five, including those aged between one and three, can be beneficial to the child, if more than just basic health and safety conditions, space and play equipment are evaluated.

The extra important ingredients are, first, the people present, how many there are in the group, and the availability of an adult with whom one can conduct a one-to-one conversation. Further, nurseries which give members of staff, including relatively young and inexperienced staff, the responsibility for a small group of children not only improve the quality of that adult's relationships with the children in the group by enhancing their autonomy and morale, but also offer increased benefits to children, because the children are offered greater opportunities to interact with those adults (Ruopp *et al.*, 1979; Tizard, 1975).

The second important ingredient is the responsiveness and sensitivity of the adults involved. Blatchford *et al.* (1982), like Tizard (1986), emphasize this prerequisite in staff. Their study of children's transitions from home to group settings indicates the importance of not 'starting from scratch' as far as an individual child is concerned; one needs a sharing of information which will assist the preschool worker in easing the child's entry to the group. It is important to develop strategies designed to contribute to a smooth transition, such as enabling parents to become part of the life of the group, through prior visits with the child, individualized staggered entry, and so on. It also seems sensible to discuss the importance of helping the child develop an attachment to the teacher or supervisor, while at the same time giving reassurances that no one can possibly replace or diminish them, the parents, in the children's affections. Adults who are generally regarded as successful in practice have usually operated in this way simply as a result of experience. They may be described as adults who have transposed the behaviours described by Webb (1984) pertaining to the home setting, and adapted them for children they work with in the group setting. In other words, they may use pet names (though not necessarily infringing parental intimacy by using the home pet name), they will develop idiosyncratic behaviours with their group, and they will 'bug and nudge' children in a way which makes them feel cared for and wanted by that adult – again, a reiteration that the child is 'special'. Other aspects of this sensitivity will be adapting to the child in the 'dance' of forming and maintaining attachments, such as appropriate frequency and length of eye-contact, touching, varieties and sequencing of dialogue, differences in pitch and tone of voice, and so on. In order to behave with such high degrees of sensitivity, staff need time to observe new children and to reflect on and discuss each child's progress.

The third important ingredient is familiarity. This can prove more problematic in some group settings, due to staff shifts, turnover and absenteeism. Where possible, it is better if children can remain with the same adult worker, rather than the groups being moved around. Similarly, the functioning of different groupings of children at different playgroup sessions is not a good idea, and children should, as far as possible, meet the same children at their various sessions. Tizard argues that mother-and-toddler clubs and 'drop-in centres' may benefit parents, but are not so good for children, because they need constancy in the group of children encountered, in order to have time to form attachments.

The very fact that there is in the UK no co-ordinated coherent policy of provision for the under-fives, means that the minimum number of adults to whom a child may have begun to attach will usually be in the order of five, and from the two NFER studies (Blatchford *et al.*, 1982; Cleave *et al.*, 1982) we deduce that it is frequently the case that those adults do not collaborate in relation to the child's individual needs. The Oxford Preschool Project (Bruner, 1980) indicated that the types of setting and play activity which foster competence in young children were those where the children were in small groups with adults who had a stable influence. Further evidence for the importance of familiarity and the intimacy offered by small groupings comes from the results of Osborn and Milbank (1987), since one cohort of the children who appear to have benefited most in the long term from preschool group attendance had participated in small home playgroups.

Perhaps we might speculate that the maturity of the preschool worker is one of the key factors in helping the child attach and the parent feel confident. This maturity is reflected in such workers' easy style, openness and confidence in their role.

Conclusion

Can we conclude that a child under five is under-educated if he or she does not attend a preschool group? While wishing to endorse the opinion of Rutter (1981), Bruner (1980), Tizard (1986) and Webb (1984) that quality is essential, we would argue that, irrespective of one's view of education, be it for 'life' or more narrowly related to schooling, the evidence seems to indicate that children do benefit, rather than suffering maternal deprivation. Furthermore, Osborn and Milbank's (1987) study showed that all children who had attended some form of preschool group performed more effectively on the tests administered at ages five and ten than children who had not attended preschool provision.

What seems to be crucial for young children in any setting, is the need to feel that one or more adults care for them as individuals and that involvement is unquestionable, unconditional and enduring.

5
Myths and realities: women's work and childcare

Women, childhood and the family

The belief that throughout history mothers, or rather good mothers, have stayed at home to look after their families is a myth, similar to that suggesting childhood has always been a time of happy innocence. We seem to have derived these impressions about childhood and motherhood from the records available, and, as Hoyles (1979) and Tucker (1977) assert, most records tell us more about upper- or middle-class life, or certainly male life, than about working-class or female life. We can infer the conditions under which poor families lived, and the values and attitudes they were forced, through circumstances, to adopt, and that parents who did not train their children for work were abnegating their responsibilities – after all, the parents could die quite suddenly and quite young.

Today we tend to take for granted that childhood is an inescapable fact of life. It is only by researching historically that we find alternative views (Aries, 1962) suggesting that childhood is a social construct and a fairly recent one at that. Postman (1985) argues that childhood really began with the printing press, and he is concerned that with the iconography of television the ability to read will no longer be necessary and fade, and that children will once again be regarded as miniature adults. However, with support from the last twenty years' psychological research concerning the way children think and learn, we can still argue that babyhood and childhood are periods of growth during which children need protection.

The view that the place for a baby or child under school age is at home with its mother has been the focus of much ideological propaganda during the twentieth century, and it has made life very difficult for young mothers who were forced through financial circumstances, or those who wished to further their careers, to continue work after childbirth. There have been some areas of the UK where a woman was less likely to develop guilt feelings, either because her own family members shared in what they regarded as good childcare provision, or because they lived in an area of traditional female employment and the women gave each other moral support in refuting the myth.

There is evidence (Tilly and Scott, 1987) that women's work was very much part of the economy in pre-industrial society, when organization was home-based. It was during the Industrial Revolution that women began to move in and out of factory life because of childbirth, or as a buffer of cheap, reserve labour. During this time, negative middle-class attitudes to women's employment outside the home, in production as opposed to reproduction, began to influence the overall ideology of society. The new style of labour organization, particularly that involving heavy industry, led to a primarily male adult labour force in many areas. However, women were involved in *light* industry, in the Potteries and in the cotton and wool towns of the North of England, and this is reflected in the traditionally higher levels of nursery provision in these areas. Also, during the early years of the twentieth century, as clerical work developed, it came to be seen as possible employment for women, including some from the middle classes. Teaching, too, came to be viewed as respectable employment, favoured also as a good 'escape' route from heavy or menial toil for working-class girls, by aspiring mothers who knew all too well what the alternatives would entail (Al-Khalifa, 1988).

The traditional view of women's role as mother and primary family carer, at home, has been in part upheld implicitly by educators and policy-makers who regarded nursery education as totally and exclusively child-centred, with short hours and, more recently, with the expectation that parents (for 'parents' read 'mothers'), would be available for involvement in sessions, trips, meetings and working parties. Those under-fives in need of care facilities were to be pitied, because they were no doubt the offspring of inadequate, feckless or uncaring parents (again, for 'parents' read 'mothers'). Although I have perhaps generalized and exaggerated such attitudes in this brief description, it is difficult to dismiss the underlying ideological standpoint which has given rise to current conditions. We are now, however, fast approaching an era in which demographic changes are forcing the government and employers to recognize that there will be a desperate shortage of employees if women with children of all ages are not encouraged to participate in the workforce.

For some, the need for women in the workforce will raise a number of difficult issues, and there are certain points which traditionalists will put foward. First, it is the women who have the children, presumably because they want them, so they should accept the consequences. Even women will subscribe to this view – it is not one held exclusively by males (Martin and Roberts, 1984). Second, feminist women have abandoned their caring function and are to blame for the ills in today's society – they are being selfish. Note that it is not that men are being selfish for not helping at home. The amount of help a woman receives from her partner is related to the woman's hours of employment. Although men over-report the frequency with which they help with chores, women report that this help is less frequent than men seem to think, and men are more likely than women to expect women to take on certain chores (Witherspoon, 1988).

Third, men become feminized when they are expected to participate in housework. (I wonder what men living on their own are to do to prevent this supposedly terrible thing happening to them?) Fourth, women's labour is less efficient because they have time off to have babies, care for sick children or other family members, etc. Employers will argue that women will not be as committed as men, but research (Dex, 1985) has shown that women's attitudes to work are as varied as those of men and depend on age, life-cycle experience, education and prospects.

Despite evidence to the contrary about its history, traditionalists are also likely to cite the importance of 'the family' (presumably the stereotyped two heterosexual adults and two children) to the emotional health of future generations. Both gender and adult–child power relations come together with intensity in what Shorter (1975) calls the 'post-modern family'. He suggests that during the last quarter of the twentieth century family life has been characterized by three main criteria: instability in the life of adult couples; a 'systematic destruction of the nest'; and indifference to or rejection on the part of adolescent children of the values and family orientation of older generations. Riach's (1989) research shows that adolescents are not rejecting the idea of family life and the values associated with it, and Shorter's point about the 'systematic destruction of the nest' may simply mean that he is being made uncomfortable by women who are finally saying that previous conditions made them unhappy, so they are rearranging things, not destroying them.

Certainly there has been a marked increase in the divorce rate, and in the numbers of children involved in parental separations; there has also been an increase in both partners in unmarried couples registering the birth of their offspring, of serial marriage, of mobility in the search for work, in lone parenting. However, we must decide whether we believe that these changes do indeed mark the destruction of family life, or take the more positive and open view that it may actually be the implications of negative attitudes towards children growing up in 'alternative' families. Perhaps it is the frequent financial difficulties they face as a result of reduced support for those not conforming to what is regarded as 'normal', which could be damaging.

Women, employment and their childcare arrangements

Despite belief to the contrary, women, particularly working-class women, have always been represented in the workforce and, where it was thought that men's labour could be regarded as separate and detached, Tilly and Scott's (1987, p. 232) historical survey suggests that

> the family continued to influence the productive activity of its members ... shaped by the intersection of economy, demography and family. Specific historical contexts differ and so do the experiences, attitudes and choices women make in different situations. Women's work had to be assessed in terms of the family.

while Dex (1985, p. 1) argues that 'prior to the 1960s much research was premised on the unwritten assumption that women's economic role was unimportant'.

This means that not only was women's employment outside the home regarded as peripheral to the needs of the economy, contributing only the luxuries to family life, but also the fact that the family impinged upon the employment potential of women from all classes was taken for granted.

It has been generally assumed that attitudes to the employment of mothers have been changing since the Second World War. But surveys show that there is still a wide range of opinion on this, including those who think women with children should be at home. Women with young children have in fact been joining the labour force in increasing numbers, but in the UK they are most likely to be employed part-time (EOC, 1988). Mothers from ethnic minority groups, especially Afro-Caribbean women, are those most likely to work long hours, for poor pay and at the mercy of poor childcare arrangements (CRC, 1975; Austen *et al.*, 1984).

The development of contraception, different birth patterns, family size, family make-up and relationships – for example, serial marriage –

means that women are increasingly available for work and are more and more likely to 'invest' in the children they have, that is, they will probably wish to work to provide funds for living, and so that children can have a good education through a variety of life experiences. Additionally, we have witnessed an upswing in the number of single parents, so that more families are headed by a lone woman. This trend is well established in Britain, it is increasing in other European Community countries albeit more slowly, and the USA is ahead of us all. There payments for childcare attract tax concessions, making part-time work less favourable than full-time, and single and married women with young children make use of this – but again, women in the USA are still marginalized into 'women's' jobs.

Martin and Roberts (1984) suggest that younger women actually attach less importance to the centrality of paid employment in their lives than do older women, for whom the choice can be more of a dilemma, given the circumstances. Perhaps young women have already realized that whatever they do their prospects are limited unless they are prepared for an immense struggle, in the personal as well as the public sphere. As a result, many of them are likely to feel that children and some part-time work are in fact the easier option. They are therefore, early on, deciding to opt out of any serious employment involvement. When they subsequently do try to re-enter, or find they have to remain in the workforce because of economic circumstances, they have their worst fears confirmed. They are usually marginalized into both vertically and horizontally segregated work – that is, most will find themselves in work carried out predominantly by women (horizontal segregation), and there will be little chance of promotion, with men occupying the top jobs (vertical segregation).

The low priority given in the past to mothers and young children has encouraged attitudes in society such that workers in the field of early education and care are also marginalized, poorly paid and in many cases subject to conditions of service which would not be tolerated by a male workforce. To a great extent, this has also been due to dependency of this field on the demand for female employment and what working women are able to pay, in the case of childminders, or demand, in the case of local authority nursery provision.

Leaving early childhood provision to market forces means, first, that women are left to decide if they will go back to or continue work, since their partners usually see any necessary payment as coming out of the woman's salary. Further, women are expected to take sole responsibility for the consequences (Brannen and Moss, 1988). The market forces approach means that children do not have any basic rights to care and education of recognized good quality. Cohen (1988) suggests that over two-thirds of childcare arrangements made by working mothers involve a relative or the child's father, and that many are left unsupervised when the care arrangement fails. This is the result of the current 'policy' of leaving childcare arrangements to parents themselves. Despite an attempt in the House of Lords in July 1989 to gain time for unemployed mothers offered work to secure appropriate care arrangements for children, the proposed, family-focused amendment to legislation was defeated by the Conservative government.

The consequence of these factors is that mothers do not enjoy an equal right to access to family-appropriate employment and they are marginalized into part-time work, short or unsocial hours, low pay, lack of promotion prospects, and lack of in-service training (see Beechey, 1986; Beechey and Perkins, 1987; Dex, 1985; Fogarty *et al.*, 1981; Jenson *et al.*, 1988; EOC, 1988). For those young families where the mother 'chooses' to stay at home, research (Brown and Harris, 1978) shows that mental illness is more prevalent among mothers who are isolated at home with their children. This seems to destroy the argument that women who go out to work are likely to crack under the strain. The strain for many working mothers is indeed great, but it can be the wider relationships and the sense of self-worth engendered by working which maintains the mother's mental health.

The net result is that the UK may be losing out because skilled and professional women workers are discouraged from participating in the labour market; because children may be receiving less than adequate care, whether they are with their own mother, who may suffer from depression, or because they attend a form of care which does not seek to be educative in the way which may be essential to enable them to develop their potential. Children whose mothers do work, yet who experience this as a positive valuable process, involving opportunities for learning how to learn, how to live in a caring, flexible, accepting community in their early years, may ultimately repay the cost of their educare to society through their own adult contributions, though this is certainly not the only argument for providing such a service. The main arguments are that children have a right to be educated, to achieve their potential, and that women have a right to equality of opportunity.

In making conclusions and recommendations based on her research concerning services and policies for childcare and equal opportunities in the UK, Cohen (1988) draws attention to the fact that sex discrimination legislation alone cannot redress the balance, and that complementary social policies are essential. However, even if a social policy relating to women's rights to employment were developed, with the inclusion of educare facilities for their children, it would probably have little effect unless a legal right were enshrined in statute, for example, similar to the right to health and education services, (George and Wilding, 1985). Owing to the difficulties faced by working mothers, they are likely to find that their potential lifetime earnings are reduced by half as a result of having children, whereas fatherhood is unlikely to cause a ripple in male employment experience or earnings.

Thus, mothers who work outside the home in current circumstances are likely to be underemployed (in terms of their abilities), undervalued, and ultimately, demoralized, suffering through conflict, either at home if chores are left undone, or at work. Most will receive little or no assistance with housework (Brannen and Moss, 1988), and, as already stated, most men questioned believed that the woman makes the choice whether or not she should return to work and she therefore must shoulder the consequences, from finding any money for childcare payments to ensuring all the household chores are still performed to the same standard as before. In other words, in order to maintain a contented and happy home life, women must try to be adept at keeping all the balls in the air. It is hardly surprising that most remain in the lower grades of their profession, partly from prejudice, partly because they value their relationships and are sensitive to the emotional needs of their partners and children. Women also seem to see work and home in symbiosis. Men do not appear to have this problem – they go out to work to enhance life at home through their earnings, but work itself rarely appears to be influenced by life elsewhere. Women, on the other hand, while keen and committed during their working hours, sometimes need to make sure they leave work on time so that they get the shopping on the way home, or in the evening, make sure the children have clean clothes for school, or find time in the week to buy a new pair of shoes. Unfortunately, workers' commitment is sometimes judged by the amount of time they are on the premises, rather than by their effectiveness. In order to function as well as possible and sustain a healthy relationship between both spheres of their lives, women are likely to choose work which is limited to known hours, or flexible enough that they can take tasks home with them.

Future prospects and changing attitudes

Will the European Community shame the UK government into acting? Moss's (1988) report, indicating the relatively poor levels of preschool provision available to the children of working parents, and the implications for the UK's equal opportunities policy, should have done that. However, any radical change to the situation seems unlikely. The

Conservative Party does have a group known as the 'Ministerial Group on Women', looking at 'women's issues'. It is chaired by John Patten and consists of ministers from twelve other government departments – only two are women. However, Conservative rhetoric about preserving the integrity of the family will mean some conflict in relation to providing childcare facilities needed to encourage women to remain in the workforce when they have children.

A Labour government coming to power, according to its manifesto, would mean better state provision of nurseries, and a possible prioritizing of an increase in the numbers of those training to be nursery teachers. Whether this will result in educare or traditional school hours is not clear. Although an increase in the number of nursery teachers would be welcomed, it may not serve children and their mothers, unless there is collaboration between services.

In order to entice precious future workers into teaching, especially into a sector which has always been the Cinderella of the service as far as pay and promotion is concerned, there would probably have to be mechanisms to increase status and pay. If parents were helped to understand the special role of the nursery teacher, the desperate need for those parents in the workforce would put them in a very powerful position to insist that their children receive nursery education as well as high-quality care – from trained teachers working in collaboration with other trained, early childhood workers, offering educare.

But in the end, when the need for workers declines, whether through an upturn in the birthrate or technological innovations, what then? Will we find that attitudes and ideology relating to gender have remained, underneath it all, the same? Will our daughters have to fight the same battles as our mothers, contemporaries and we ourselves have fought? In this attempt to juggle career and family, will they be made to feel guilty and inadequate, not only by partner, employer, childless and male colleagues, but also by the very people we would expect to offer support, mostly working mothers themselves – nursery workers? We must all examine our attitudes and values and ask what messages we transmit, what beliefs we manifest in our dealings with working mothers. If we do not, we risk transmitting attitudes which will influence the growing consciousness of the children we teach, both girls and boys.

Riach's (1989) research among teenage girls in the UK and Australia demonstrates that, despite their own childhood experiences, they have unreal expectations about their futures. They believe they will be able to pursue top careers, have a husband and family and still manage to spend endless time at their children's disposal. What Riach suggests is family education for all pupils in their mid-teens, so that they can consider these issues. All too often, courses in 'childcare' have been provided for those regarded as low-achieving girls, and they have focused on, quite literally, childcare, rarely touching on gender issues and women's careers.

We need to examine the possibility of changing the attitudes of women, men, and of society as a whole. Women need to be assertive about what their own and their children's rights are in a democratic society. We should support women colleagues in their professional development and encourage more women to become involved in work on public bodies, and in politics. We need more educare support for women and children and we should demand that those who organize unions, political groups, and so on, become sensitive to the way in which, for example, early evening meetings exclude women.

Men, as partners, must realize the need for them to support their child's mother in her career by helping more in the home, and in accepting that decisions about maternal employment and the search for educare are the responsibility of both partners.

Men, as employers (some are female but most are male), need to ask themselves whether they are positive about their commitment to ensuring that female employees are not the victims of discrimination and that they themselves are not losing talented workers. So often employers have used women's responsible attitudes towards their children as a stick with which they can beat them into submission, offering paltry pay in exchange for what they insist is their accommodation to the needs of those women to work shorter, or so called 'anti-social' hours. A young mother who is offered the 'choice' of working five hours during the day, or five hours from 4.30 to 9.30 p.m. may well feel she should be grateful. When her child is under school age she can accept the evening work, so that her partner, assuming she has one, will be the evening carer, and when her child reaches school age she may opt for the daytime hours, to fit in with those of school. Of course there are positive points to such arrangements, for those who can make them: the father spends some time with the child and the mother may feel that he, along with grandparents and other close relatives, are her first choice as home-based alternatives to herself. But what happens when other family members do not live nearby, or the father is absent, or his work makes heavy demands or requires him to be flexible, at a time in his life when he is likely to be attempting to develop his own career? Some employers do not capitalize on women workers' vulnerability but there is much research evidence (see, for example, EOC, 1988) to show that women working part-time are rarely offered in-service training, rarely gain promotion, are paid low rates and remain on the lowest rungs of their career structure. In countries where parenthood is taken seriously by state and employers, maternity/paternity and sick-child leave are simply part of a recognition that changed work patterns aimed at helping both parents perform all their roles well are likely to foster a positive and productive workforce, rather than an anxious, driven one. The benefits to society in general seem obvious – workers who can concentrate on the task in hand when at their workplace, and a future generation which is ensured high self-esteem, because it realizes the importance society attaches to its well-being.

Society as a whole needs to ensure the education of future generations about equal opportunities; enjoyment of children; exploitation; 'divide and rule' of some employers and exclusion of women from 'male' trades. The trade unions could be an important part of this support network, yet they have all too often worked for men against women. They have reacted in fear when a particular type of work has begun to be infiltrated by women, because what has happened traditionally to jobs which have become feminized is that the work is relabelled and devalued, so that any men remaining in this field then suffer a loss of status and pay.

Additionally, the view that part-time work is somehow aberrant, and that the traditional (male) workday pattern of hours is 'normal' must be challenged. There may well be many men, as well as women, who would opt to work flexibly, or to shorten their day, in order to spend more time with their small children.

Perhaps it is only by working together, as women, working mothers ourselves in most cases, with the mothers who need education and care facilities, and with men who have come to understand that life could be different and that there are alternative ways of organizing work – inside the home and out – that we can achieve a fairer, more equitable society.

The symbiotic relationship between parent and child – in most cases with the mother as central – means that we cannot ignore the issue of mothers' employment outside the home. In some countries the attitudes, ideology and economy may mean that the participation of women with young children in the workforce is viewed positively, that the rights of mothers are not seen as conflicting with those of the child. In many, countries however, despite various sources of pressure on women to take up paid employment, there is still an underlying ideology of motherhood and family responsibility which results in an unfair burden of work and of guilt being laid on women.

The myth of the 'mother made conscious'

The ideology of family in which the gender roles are so tightly defined that the mother is seen as more or less exclusively responsible for meeting family members' needs, as the principal carer, is also manifest in the attitudes towards early childhood educators. Nursery teachers and infant teachers, are, in the words of Carolyn Steedman (1988), 'the mother made conscious' – she has to be the perfect, middle-class idealization of a mother. Such role prescription is not useful – it places a strain on the relationship between mothers and teachers, partly because it is as if the teacher is expected to correct their 'parental misdemeanours', partly because the relationship with such a 'mother' will not be one based on partnership.

Additionally, by being defined as a carer, she is denied acceptance as a highly expert professional, with much to offer teacher colleagues who work with older children. As Steedman argues, the message is that you do not have to be very clever to become an early childhood educator.

I would not wish early years teachers to stop caring, to stop loving the children they teach, but unless they are rigorous and articulate about the complexity of the tasks they perform, their work will continue to go unrecognized and unrewarded. Early years teachers are currently subject to the same horizontal and vertical segregation as others engaged in professions and occupations deemed to be the sphere of women, and as a result they, too, have been marginalized.

EDUCARE FOR THE UNDER-FIVES

6
Continuity

In recent years there has been much support for the view that young children thrive if they experience 'continuity' in their lives, and that 'discontinuities' will cause difficulties.

The first transition

In her discussion of the research study of Blatchford et al. (1982), Clark (1988) suggests that while it alerted practitioners to some of the issues they should address in fostering smooth entry to group experience for young children and their parents, it left certain important questions to be tackled by subsequent project teams. For example, were the children undergoing the most severe difficulties at this stage also likely to be those who would experience alienation and dislocation throughout their school careers? Further, if it is possible to identify such children prior to the initial group membership, could strategies be found which would prevent such waste and misery?

Unfortunately, there has been very little research into the adjustments babies and young children must make before they reach the primary school stage. Apart from the work by Blatchford et al. (1982) on children's first move out of the home to group experience, the kind of evidence on which we must rely comes from research which focuses on attachment (see Chapter 4), rather than on the processes which are involved in moving children confidently between one carer and another.

Some of the large-scale research studies of the 1970s noted incidentally certain aspects of children's first months in a preschool group. For example, the Keele study (Hutt et al., 1989) found that three-year-olds spend, on average, about a third of their time during their first six months in the group, irrespective of type of provision, watching what is going on around them. After that period, their level of involvement in, for example, fantasy play, tends to rise and the proportion of time looking around or watching others is reduced. The way in which such data may be helpful to practitioners is to signal to them the importance of making observations of how children are spending their time at different points during their period of attendance. At the beginning, high levels of looking round and watching others will probably be regarded as perfectly 'normal' – after all, this is what we adults do when we go to a new place. On the other hand, children who, after several months' attendance, are still reticent about engaging in activities, 'cruising' and avoiding contact with either other children or adults, probably need 'investigation'. Close relationships with parents would help in such a case, although it must be admitted that, from anecdotal evidence, children who caused concern to parents and staff in this way have sometimes divulged their often powerful preschool inhibitions only in later life. Maybe a set of retrospective case studies would tease out some of the underlying causes of preschoolers' anxieties or reasons for disaffection.

Transition between preschool establishments

We have insufficient evidence of the extent to which some children may be attending a confusing multiplicity of forms of provision, in some cases concurrently, in others serially, as parents move areas, jobs, or because each type of provision offers different facilities. For example, children in many areas will probably attend a parent-and-toddler club, then a playgroup, and, where available, move on to a nursery school or class before entry to the reception class of a primary school. The reason for the move from playgroup to nursery class is likely to be due to parents' belief that this will prepare their children for 'the big school' (Ward, 1982). However, it must also be remembered that maintained nursery places are free of charge, while playgroup sessions are not, and a nursery place is likely to be for every day of the week, not sporadic sessions. Even the brightest four-year-olds will have difficulty in making a mental ordering of their weekly pattern of attendance and will ask each morning if it is their day to go to playgroup, when daily attendance, Monday to Friday, is not possible.

For children experiencing concurrent attendance at more than one form of preschool provision the situation is probably even less satisfactory. Some children, perhaps those with a part-time nursery school place, may attend another group, perhaps a playgroup, during the afternoons. In another case, where parents think them ready to attend for five sessions per week but where there is only playgroup provision, children may be registered with two different playgroups in order to achieve such attendance. A child moving from one preschool group to another in this way will be very unlikely to experience continuity, since in some cases parents may try to keep their activities secret, so as not to offend the sensitivities of the different playgroup staff and not to appear to have divided loyalties.

Possibly the only type of provision in which concurrent attendance at another is seen as positive and is developed in a carefully monitored way is the use of groups, whether statutory or voluntary, by caring child-minders, who may be members of the child's own family, nannies, or those who are paid to mind children in their own (the minders') homes. It seems probable that home-based minding may be a form of provision which increases dramatically with the need for women to remain in the workforce. The need for those in other forms of provision to foster co-operative links with this voluntary group is imperative and more research will be needed to study the essential ingredients of links of this nature which prove beneficial to the children they serve. It is only through such strategies that we can ensure continuity, smooth transitions and overlaps, rather than confusion and fear bred by unfamiliarity.

Transition from home or preschool to the reception class

When children go on to enter the infant reception class they may come from a range of settings. A number of studies (for example, Jackson, 1979; Cleave *et al.*, 1982; Hamilton, 1984; Willes, 1983; Barrett, 1986; Stevenson, 1987; Ghayle and Pascal, 1988; Hutt *et al.*, 1989) provide valuable pointers concerning the discontinuities between nursery or home and the reception class. First, children entering reception class experience a significant alteration in the availability of adult attention, since there may be one teacher to a class of more than twenty four- or five-year-olds. Second, the reception class may operate a very different regime from that experienced by children either at home or in a nursery setting, with a reduction in choice of activity, availability of activities, outdoor play space, sessions and equipment. This includes changes in teaching style, changes in curriculum, and changes in ethos.

Hutt *et al.* (1989) were surprised to discover that children they observed in reception class appeared to have gained little advantage over their peers from having attended nursery school. Their behaviour in general became homogenized, as they learned to ' "toe the line", in a way which is as unfamiliar to the ex-nursery school children, as it is to the children who come straight from home' (Hutt *et al.,* 1989, p. 203).

However, in a study by Jowett and Sylva (1986), children who had attended nurseries where learning was effected through 'guided play' were found to have advantages over classmates who had experienced other forms of provision.

In order to provide continuity in those aspects of experience which will otherwise cause children and their parents distress, it is important for all concerned to be aware of the many and complex influences so as to be able to offer some continuity of experience and expectation to children moving from one setting to another. Among those factors identified by Barrett (1986) as affecting whether or not there will be a match or a (wasteful) mismatch between children's preschool experiences and the expectations of the primary school were personal history; the financial and physical and social environment; personal, cultural and societal values; the level of understanding of child development, learning and schooling; and the future possibilities of all the key figures in the child's life.

Chapter 10 stresses the adult's role in helping children make sense of their world. It is suggested that fostering children's ability to disembed (Donaldson, 1978) learning, in other words, to extract from its context the concept which has been learned and to be able to apply it in other situations, is an essential feature of the style adopted by a reflective teacher. To put children in a situation which is totally different from their earlier experiences amounts to decontextualization; what we should be promoting is *re*contextualization (Walkerdine, 1982), that is, building on previous learning. Willes (1983) study of children being transformed into pupils highlights the way in which the time spent on some of the formalized procedures of schooling may be wasted at this stage. One wonders if the achievement of greater 'match' between the nursery and reception class in Jowett and Sylva's (1986) study may have been due to the fact that the reception class staff in question did foster recontextualization, building profitably on the children's experiences in nursery, but being less able to do so for the children with playgroup experience for some reason.

Gentle admissions procedures, pre-entry school visits by children, with parental support, explanatory booklets, talks and videos are all important. But so, too, are visits back and forth by staff from preschool settings and the reception class teacher, and observation of children in their preschool settings by that teacher. Evaluation of a school from the point of view of its youngest pupils can result in an awareness of the need for changes in ethos, resourcing and teaching styles by primary schools. In some cases the latter points are difficult to deal with unless the reception class teacher has the support of the headteacher, and support in the form of funding for extra staff and resources from the LEA. Further, the reception class teacher needs the understanding of colleagues and parents, for pressure to behave in particular ways can be strong, for example, to bring children into full-time attendance before they are ready, to over-emphasize reading, writing and pages of sums.

This discontinuity in ethos between the majority of preschool settings and many reception classes is especially poignant where children of barely four are being admitted. Zigler (1987) argues from American research evidence that formal schooling situations are not beneficial, even to middle-class children, some of whom may appear academically and socially precocious and able to cope. He warns that as a response to the need for more parents (that is to say, mothers) as workers, taking children early into school, rather than providing nursery programmes, is dangerous and inappropriate.

A further issue related to the admission of children to reception class at the start of the school year in which they are five is the 'knock-on' effect on the preschool groups. An annual intake of three-year-olds to a nursery, despite gentle admissions strategies, is likely to be a daunting prospect without the 'old hands', the four-year-olds, to initiate them into the group. The other side of this 'coin' is the reduction in opportunities for these children, the older preschoolers, to take on the role of elder, caring friend. It was a blossoming which delighted many of us in the days when it was widespread practice for 'new' children to start nursery each term, after others had moved on to 'big school'.

Considering the variety of preschool settings a group of children could have attended, is it reasonable to expect a reception class teacher to achieve continuity of experience for her charges? Given also that in some of those settings the children may not have been encouraged to learn through guided play, would we want the reception class teacher to adopt such a facilitative, rather than didactic, style of working? Jowett and Sylva's (1986) study indicates that the best type of setting on which such a teacher might base her new regime would be that of the nursery school, rather than the playgroup, and, equally, studies of formal reception class experience indicate the need to adopt the more flexible, guided play methods (see, for example, Stevenson, 1987; Bennett and Kell, 1989).

Watt (1987) argues that the suggestion that reception class practice be modelled on the nursery school is sensible as long as that nursery school provides 'good' nursery education, that is, children should experience 'familiarity' (continuity of adult and child associates), 'responsiveness' (sensitive adults who respond spontaneously to the child, whom they see as an individual), 'attachment' (reciprocal adult–child and child–child bonding), the development of self-esteem, positive attitudes to learning, and opportunities to plan and to carry out those plans successfully.

It seems ironic that after many years of primary schools expecting nurseries to tailor the children to their needs (many nurseries 'feed' a number of primary schools, each with differing expectations), the evidence of researchers is pointing in the opposite direction. Some of these difficulties stem from the fact that nursery teachers and infant teachers have different aims and objectives for their pupils (Clark *et al.*, 1984; Wallace, 1985). The problem is that unless the status of early years teachers is enhanced, endorsing good nursery practice, either locally (through local authority advisory services) or nationally (through government intervention or through the inspectorate), the lot of young children in primary schools will remain unaffected. Similarly, while nursery practitioners allow colleagues teaching in primary and secondary schools, parents, politicians and others, to continue in the belief that they 'just play with' and 'mind' young children, they are in part to blame for these discrepancies.

Efforts to enhance continuity

At a conference held by EC ministers in 1981, an optimistic statement was issued stressing the value each member nation placed on early childhood education, from age three to eight, the importance of co-ordination of all preschool services, equal opportunities and the need for policies to prevent colonization of preschool provision by the primary school system (Van der Eyken, 1982).

To some extent the UK has already seen an erosion of that statement's aims in the increase in under-fives in reception classes. A further erosion could result from an inappropriate, top-down implementation of the National Curriculum. The Education Minister, Mrs Angela Rumbold, has already made public her view that nursery staff may commence the National Curriculum if a child is 'ready'. While not wishing to appear to recommend that a child be held back from educational achievements, my point here would be that no consideration has been given to what might precede the National Curriculum, nor has recognition been given to the fact that a good nursery teacher would in any case be helping a child work on achieving tasks matched to that child's individual stage and ability. This might well include activities documented in National Curriculum programmes of study, since this is what happened before the National

Curriculum was devised. However, many nursery practitioners would draw back from the idea of pushing a child on, through the demands of activities set out in narrowly defined subject divisions, rather than in developmental or cross-curricular fashion.

Returning to the meeting of EC Ministers, their intention was that all European children should experience continuity of curriculum between the ages of three and eight. In this country this is impossible at present, first, because under-fives are in such a wide variety of settings with differently trained staff, and second because the early years curriculum is only being considered after the curriculum for 5–16-year-olds. A national curriculum as entitlement has wide support, but the implications for achieving such a curriculum for children under five are fraught with difficulty.

In some local authorities (for example, Grampian, 1987) there have been attempts to make transition from home to school, or from preschool to reception class, as benign as possible, through policy statements, working party reports, practical advice and courses for primary teachers. This sensitization is vital, but so, too, is the need for time, for each primary school team to discuss its young newcomers, to visit homes and preschool groups, to plan room use and equipment, and to help parents understand the crucial nature of school entry and its potentially lifelong influence.

So, is discontinuity bad for children?

Discontinuity has been given a bad 'press' because we tend to equate it with the idea that young children need consistency of adult contact and consistency of treatment. Cleave *et al.* (1982) summed up the essential features of what is meant here by suggesting that what children need is compatibility rather than 'sameness'.

This would be corroborated by findings from the United States, where discontinuity between home and preschool in terms of role expectations and different interactions was not found to be problematic for young children; in fact, such discontinuities added spice to their lives. Long and Garduque (1987, p. 87) suggest it may teach them 'to adjust to social demands they will encounter as they move out of the home into the wider social world'. Even where parents hold different attitudes and beliefs from those held by teachers, where discontinuity could be expected to have a harmful or problematic effect, parents in general saw this as an important learning situation.

What these authors suggest is that we should be sensitive to potential discontinuities in children's experience and evaluate their effects.

Perhaps children who never experience discontinuity do not develop the ability to cope with it when they meet it in later life. By offering children opportunities to experience 'stimulation' rather than 'shock' (Cleave *et al.*, 1982), through appropriate challenges, we are preserving their excitement at surmounting rites of passage. It would be sad to deprive children of such life steps by making every boundary between stages so blurred it becomes invisible – let us ensure that all our children pass each milestone with exhilaration, joy and a sense of achievement.

7
Equal opportunities?

In order to consider the possibility that children under five may be under-educated because of a system in which inequalities exist, it is first of all necessary to examine the ways in which inequalities are defined and thought to operate.

On 20 November 1959, the General Assembly of the United Nations ratified, without any member nation's dissent, a statement declaring the Rights of the Child. The rights agreed upon include 'the right to equality, regardless of race, colour, religion, sex or nationality' and, in November 1989, the United Nations Convention, to supplement the Declaration, was submitted to the UN General Assembly, after ten years of drafting.

The term 'equality' is one which has generated some debate. In the UK today equality of opportunity tends to be regarded as a democratic right. Equality of opportunity is not equal – meaning 'the same' – provision, nor does it imply that there will necessarily be equal outcomes. This equality debate was at its height, in relation to young children, during the 1960s when the compensatory education programmes in the United States and the UK were being widely and enthusiastically advocated as the solution to poor school achievement among working-class pupils compared to their middle-class counterparts.

Since that time we have begun to realize that there are groups of children who are being systematically disadvantaged because of their classification as female, black or working-class, or a combination of these categories. There are strong arguments in favour of the added inclusion of children with special educational needs in this disadvantaged cohort, although in this chapter I examine the evidence for discrimination against – and therefore under-education of – children under five on the basis of their gender, race or class.

Under-education - the gender debate

From the moment of conception, the development of a human male is different from that of a female. Hutt (1972) lists the ways in which the male foetus is more vulnerable to accidents, and, once born, the male is more prone to early death, disease, and the effects of dietary deficiency. She also describes how girls' structural development facilitates their earlier behavioural ability, for example, to crawl and walk. By the age of three weeks, boys are generally more fretful and irritable and sleep less than their more pliant female counterparts. As a result, male babies tend to be treated differently by their carers, gaining a greater degree of attention. Other biological factors which demonstrate sexual differences between very young babies are the female's superior responsiveness to auditory stimuli and the male's preference for visual stimulation. From work carried out over twenty years ago by Taylor (1969), we know that the brain develops faster in girls than boys, although this does not rule out wide variations between one girl and another, or one boy and another – indeed, since sex differences are differences between the average score for each sex, the total array of scores for the two sexes will overlap. As Meadows (1986) points out, males, on average, may be more assertive and forceful, yet our present Prime Minister, although genetically female, displays considerable assertiveness and forcefulness. It seems unlikely that physical differences of the types described above should predestine girls and women to be under-represented in the fields of maths and science, for example.

We become emotionally committed to the gender role ascribed to us at a very early age, (Kessler and McKenna, 1985), so that by the age of three most children know what is expected of them, as members of a sexual group and of their counterparts. Dunn's (1987) observations of mothers and their two-year-olds indicate that girls are taken into their mothers' confidence at this early age over the emotional complications of life relating to human feelings. In a discussion of the structure and development of childhood gender roles, Archer (1989) reports that from the age of 15 months, children can distinguish between male and female, and make 'gender-appropriate' toy choices.

Evidence supporting teachers' claims that parents and the media have caused children to develop stereotyped behaviour patterns during the preschool years, with fathers differentiating to a greater extent than mothers (Rubin *et al.,* 1974; Campos *et al.,* 1983; Huston, 1983; Block, 1984), also shows that these parental effects persist throughout childhood. Additionally, the research indicates that when parents' own behaviour is less stereotyped, as one would expect, the children's behaviour reflects this and that girls who display androgynous characteristics and expectations tend to have mothers who are pursuing a career (Etaught, 1974; Gold and Andres, 1978; Block, 1984). Toys bought for children (Davie *et al.*, 1984) demonstrate parental discrimination, as anyone who carries out a survey of primary school children will discover, particularly in relation to technological and construction toys. Why should it be that in a technological society in which childrearing takes up a much smaller proportion of the lives of adult females than used to be the case, we are clinging to the early ascription of gender roles?

According to Davies (1987), genderedness is complex and it is not enough for us to demonstrate to young children that they could take on non-stereotypic roles; we need to guide children towards knowing how to do this.

Unfortunately, the evidence suggests that children's experiences at school reinforce and exaggerate the development of differentiation according to gender stereotypes. Whyte (1983) argues that girls are more responsive to teacher demands than to those of the tasks set, seeking to please, and that although girls under five are, generally, likely to be intellectually superior to boys, they already retreat from competition, react negatively to perceived failure, and lack confidence. In the words of Spender and Sarah (1980), they are already 'learning to lose'.

The ways in which adults working with young children have been encouraging the continuation of the 'boys will be boys' situation and its implications have been observed and documented in a number of studies (for example, Clarricoates, 1978; Ebbeck, 1985; French and French, 1984; Hartley, 1980; May and Ruddock, 1983; Mullin *et al.*, 1986). What these studies show is that both girls and boys are missing out. The boys are being taught to compete, to be aggressive, to dominate proceedings, and to think that if they fail at a task it is not their fault but due to some extraneous cause. The girls, on the other hand, are learning that there are certain abilities and skills which it is inappropriate for them to demonstrate, that they should please others, be quiet, clean, and helpful, and that if they fail at a task the cause is their own inadequacy. Should a child cross these demarcation lines – a quiet, compassionate boy might, for instance show no interest in the block corner – that child is, perhaps unwittingly, treated as odd.

Mullin *et al.* (1986) state that in one of the classes they observed there were four very quiet boys, children the authors described as 'invisible', children whose teachers would name them last if asked to list their class from memory. Yet in that same class there were only four girls who were not quiet. May and Ruddock (1983) found that when asked to complete observation diaries, the teachers in their study named boys twice as often as girls and Ebbeck (1985) replicated the results obtained by Spender and Sarah (1980), finding that teachers of preschool children, similarly to their colleagues teaching older pupils, had 60 per cent of their interactions with boys.

Some recent studies (e.g. Pollard, 1985) of primary school children show that the situation is far from the simple one it was assumed to be a few years ago. Walden and Walkerdine (1982) demonstrated, in their transcripts of nursery conversations, that certain girls were skilfully manoeuvring play situations, that they would take up all types of play normally denoted as male as long as they were not discouraged from doing so, and, further, that they showed considerable mathematical ability in some cases. It may be that in subsequent years these girls will find it politic to disguise their skills and that their teachers may misinterpret the ways in which they operate, so that their mathematical abilities are under-rated.

Practitioners (see, for example, EOC, 1982; ILEA, 1986a; Witcher, 1985) who have tried to develop both their own awareness and different approaches in order to allow children to develop as individuals yet still feel comfortable as girls or boys suggest that we should note the following issues:

- Is the staff sensitive to gender stereotyping?
- Is the staff structure patriarchal?
- Do boys dominate space and interaction? (If so, the hidden message that boys are more important and more interesting is being conveyed.)
- Are children given stereotypic tasks? (For example, do older boys help with the youngest children as much as the older girls are asked to do?)
- Are girls encouraged to use technological equipment? (They are likely to lack confidence if they have not experienced this type of equipment at home, so a vicious cycle is set up.)
- Are parents involved so that they understand and support the changes?
- Are teachers and other workers aware of the subtleties of interactions in which the hidden agenda may be operating? (Observations show that we rebuke boys more loudly, more often and more sharply than we do girls, thereby reinforcing the notion that boys are expected to be unruly.)
- To undo the already fixed expectations of children we must present them with real people who perform non-stereotypical work – for example, the male nurse – and we must encourage them to engage in play activities from which they are apt to shy away. We can also search out books and pictures which challenge such fixed roles.

- By observing each other and children, we can alter our practices in appropriate ways. For example, if the boys dominate the choice of outdoor play equipment, we might allow the girls to go outside first or separately for a while, until they reach a point where they are sufficiently confident with the equipment to be assertive (see McGill, 1986).

As with all the issues debated in this chapter, it is the adult's perceptions which are crucial. We have all been brought up in a society in which we were educated to adopt a particular gender stereotype. Walkerdine (1984) argues that women nursery teachers in particular are in a catch-22 situation if they adopt a child-centred approach, for it may mean they tolerate abusive and dominant behaviour from their boy pupils. This will only be so, however, if the teacher accepts the view that 'child-centred' means that the adult has no role in assisting the child to make certain choices and pursue certain activities, and if the adult also accepts the view that 'boys will be boys' means that males are by nature rough, aggressive and abusive of females. Such a teacher is damaging not only the girls who may take her as a role model but also the boys who are forming relationships in the nursery which will serve as models for their later life.

Under-education – the race debate

The Rampton Report (DES, 1981a) concluded that the under-achievement of West Indian (as they were then called) children in British schools was rooted in experiences during the preschool years. Following this interim report, the Swann Committee (DES, 1985b) attributed the under-achievement of children from minority groups to the relative lack of appropriate preschool provision, language differences between home and school, young children's perceptions concerning the effects of racial classification, and institutional racism – including the ways in which teachers' behaviour towards certain children is determined by attitudes the teachers themselves have absorbed as members of a post-colonial British society.

The lack of sufficient appropriate provision for young children from ethnic minority backgrounds operates in a number of ways. According to the CRC (1975), the shortfall in demand for nursery places hits minority groups particularly hard, since ethnic minority mothers are more likely to take employment outside the home, with long hours and low pay. This in turn means that such parents need long hours of care for their children, at low cost or, preferably, free. However, playgroups in particular, whether hall- or home-based, are unlikely to cater for the needs of ethnic minority children (Osborn and Milbank, 1987), with 68 per cent of hall and 75 per cent of home playgroups having no Asian or Afro-Caribbean children attending. Although their data were collected in 1975, and the groupings and terminology used would now be different, Osborn and Millbank's (1987) survey shows that, in the maintained sector, Afro-Caribbeans favoured day nursery provision and Asians nursery schools or classes. Jackson and Jackson (1979) estimated that about 50,000 children of West Indian origin were being left with unregistered minders each day. At that time, this was half the estimated total of such children in the UK. Similarly, Osborn and Milbank (1987) found that Afro-Caribbean women were more likely to be single parents, with 56.8 per cent working outside the home, 31.8 per cent full-time. Since a further 18 per cent had worked at some time during their child's preschool lifetime, the total is nearer 75 per cent, compared with 45.2 per cent of white mothers. Although Asian mothers are less likely to take outside employment, when they do it is likely to be full-time work. A study by the ILEA (1982) showed that Afro-Caribbean parents in London were more likely to use day nurseries or childminders, and that 24 per cent of London Asian parents did not seek any form of preschool provision for their children. The CRC (1975) report had emphasized the fact that childminders were unlikely to offer adequate provision. If they were white they failed to meet the cultural and linguistic needs of the children – and one must ask oneself whether their own socialization equipped them to work positively with black children. Even if the minders were black, the other limits imposed on minders generally, through lack of funding, training grants, and so on, still applied. They were unlikely at that time to be able to offer a high standard of care due to their own economic constraints, environmental conditions and the lack of support services. Allen (1976) drew attention to the main problems posed to ethnic minority parents in leaving their children with minders. Minders were unable to use the mother-tongue of the child and there was likely to be a lack of books which fostered a positive self-image. Those which were provided often included negative images (Little Black Sambo, for example) or were racist by omission – Jackson (1979) mentions the failure of birthday card manufacturers to depict young children as anything other than whites with (almost always) blue eyes.

It seems unfair to lay these criticisms at the feet of minders, since we were no doubt all of us in early childhood provision unthinkingly guilty of the same dereliction of duty to minority group children. The question we must ask ourselves is what we are doing about the situation now we know the evidence.

During the 1960s and 1970s the importance of preschool group attendance for children from homes in which a language different from English was spoken was seen as paramount, so that the child could be schooled in English and thus not be a 'problem' for the reception class teacher. Of course, the argument ran a little differently from this, it was all for the benefit of the child, and Asian mothers, in particular, were also encouraged to attend language classes. The Bullock Report (DES, 1975) warned that Britain was falling behind in failing to capitalize on the advantages and importance of bilingualism. The report addressed the issue of minority languages, stating:

> No child should be expected to cast off the language and culture of the home as he crosses the school threshold, nor to live and act as though school and home represent two totally separate and different cultures which have to be kept apart (DES, 1975, para. 20.5).

Recent work suggests that becoming bilingual can have a positive effect on cognitive growth. What Cummins (1976) describes as 'the process of objectification' is similar to Donaldson's (1978) 'disembedding language' in which children, to be successful in the education system, must be capable of turning language and thought in upon themselves, to direct their own thought processes in order that they are able to choose what they will say – in other words, they must be capable of manipulating symbols, and for preschool children those symbols will, in the main, be oral language. For a bilingual child such awareness may indeed occur earlier, as Vygotsky (1962) suggested: to be able to express the same thought in two languages would probably lead the child to see the mother-tongue as one system among many and thus to view its phenomena under more general categories, so that the child would become aware of linguistic operations. By making use of the mother-tongue, teachers not only build on the child's already present concept development, but also they reflect back to the child and the family the value they attach to the child's cultural heritage and enhance the learning opportunities of all the children in the group by making them aware of language systems.

Ming's (1984) survey for the CRE highlights the blindness of the UK educational establishment, which has so long ignored the richness of experience available to all children through community languages being accorded their rightful place in the school. Early examples of minority ethnic parents providing classes outside mainstream education are Hebrew and Polish mother-tongue teaching, and since the early 1970s there have been many other such voluntary classes. The Chinese parents interviewed for the CRE survey gave, overwhelmingly, the maintenance of cultural identity and tradition as their main aim in sending their children to such classes and they expressed the wish for Chinese to be taught as a mainstream subject in ordinary schools. Edwards's (1986) work on patois among black British youth raises a number of issues concerning dialect as a form of bilingualism. She found, contrary to popular belief, that the use of dialect did not necessarily reflect hostility on the part of the speaker to mainstream white society. Attitudes to that society may affect the frequency of use, and indeed it is an assertion of black identity which whites may interpret as threatening but which may simply be chosen in certain situations to communicate a group ethos of familiarity and warmth. Use of patois was not restricted to low achievers and Edwards suggests that its use in a formal situation may be an act of defiance. Some teachers have suggested that patois, like mother-tongues, should be adopted in school, but others (such as Stone, 1981) assert that such initiatives are doomed to failure because they are simply ways of emasculating black culture and offering black pupils an education which will not give them the skills they will need in their future lives in mainstream society. Carby (1980) does not expect the adoption of dialect to eradicate racism from schools but Edwards herself is more hopeful that at least the development of greater awareness of language and the myths which surround minority cultures may form an element in anti-racist teaching. The National Curriculum programme of study for English reiterates the view of the Bullock Report (DES, 1975), but also insists that children should be capable of making themselves understood in a wide variety of situations.

Turning to young children's perceptions of racial differences, we find evidence from forty years ago (Clark and Clark, 1947; Goodman, 1952) that children as young as three are able to distinguish between white and non-white and, further, that they are aware of the social implications of that attribution. As one child said: 'The white people go up, the brown people go down.' For those sceptics who think society has changed since the above research was undertaken, Southwell (1984) found similar results among UK nursery children.

The issue of institutional racism, the systematic deprivation of black children of their rights, due to the prevailing attitudes in society and hence in the teaching force, must be addressed. Sarup (1986) argues that although teachers cannot redress the balance in a society in which prejudice operates a system of privilege, they can enable pupils and colleagues to develop awareness of this system at work. Coard (1971) argued that the disproportionate number of black pupils found in special schools and units was not the result of lack of intelligence (teachers may have claimed the support of Jensen (1969) in classifying black pupils as inheriting low IQ scores). Coard felt that discrimination caused the categorization of pupils into low ability groups and that these pupils had subsequently lived up (or down) to their teachers' expectations. The Fish Report (ILEA, 1985a) confirmed this tendency. Stone (1981) similarly argued that multi-cultural education was a misinterpretation of the view that black children were under-achieving because their home cultures were not reflected or valued in school. She insisted that to channel black children into ethnic arts was to disinherit them from opportunities offered by a knowledge of the white middle-class curriculum.

In a longitudinal study of London infant schools, Tizard *et al.* (1988) recently found that black children were reaching similar standards to those reached by their white classmates and that Afro-Caribbean girls were likely to be achieving higher standards in reading and writing than all other groups. However, Professor Tizard is quoted (*Times Educational Supplement*, 18 September 1987) as stating: 'There is some evidence that teachers had higher expectations of boys and a hint in the teachers' judgement of the work that they had lower expectations of black children.' This is a depressing finding, considering the fact that of all local authorities the ILEA is one which has worked most assiduously to help teachers develop anti-racist and anti-sexist practices, through courses, workshops, videos and other resources.

Perhaps the most important realization has been the need to educate white pupils in a way which will ensure their future commitment to a society in which there are equal opportunities for all, since it is white prejudice which, when coupled with power, maintains the status quo and prevents black members of society from obtaining their rights as citizens. Workers with under-fives can now turn to a number of publications and organizations for help (see CRE, 1977; ILEA, 1981; 1986a; VOLCUF, 1986; GLC, 1986; Development Education Centre, 1984; AFFOR, 1983).

There is a need for preschool workers to form positive relationships with all parents, but especially the parents of groups whose language, cultural heritage or religion may be different from their own. The Ethnic Relations Research Unit at Warwick University has investigated the thoughts and feelings of Mirpuri parents about the education of their children in inner-city primary schools; although they are generally satisfied, the parents express concern over various aspects of school life, including the experience of racial harassment (Joly, 1986).

Religious aspects of difference are often over-emphasized by those who see 'mixed race' schools as a problem. An example is the 1987 Dewsbury dispute in which a number of white parents refused to allow their children to take up places at a local middle school because its pupil population was 70 per cent Asian. The white parents claimed that they insisted on a Christian education for their children. The school they were rejecting was in fact a school controlled by the Church of England, which *was* offering a Christian education – and, in accordance with DES (1981b, 1985a) recommendations, wherever their children attended school they would be educated through a multi-cultural curriculum for life in multi-cultural Britain. The Education Reform Act 1988 included legislation concerning acts of worship. This, together with the possible refusal to grant voluntary aided status to Muslim schools when other religious sects enjoy such benefits, is questionable policy in a supposedly pluralist society.

Under-education – the class debate

Social class can be difficult to define in a meaningful way. As Rutter and Madge (1976) point out, despite the fact that many writers have emphasized the barriers to social mobility and the inheritance of the treadmill of underprivilege, even over two generations there is considerable movement. However, Rutter and Madge report that there is 'particularly limited movement at the top (and possibly the bottom) of the occupational hierarchy'.

Although by the mid-1970s there had been a reduction in the proportion of unskilled and semi-skilled workers in the population, the gap between social classes in relation to infant mortality, educational progress, economic resources, working conditions and illness persisted (Field, 1974). The increased levels of unemployment and large-scale dependency on social security benefits indicate the rising tide of disadvantage. CPAG (1987) estimates that since 1979 there has been an increase of 47 per cent in the number of people living on or below the 'poverty line' (taken as qualifying for supplementary benefit, possibly in itself wholly inadequate).

Osborn and Milbank (1987) found startling contrasts between the patterns of preschool group attendance for different social classes. They presented their results in two different forms. Taking social class to be defined by the father's occupation, they found that 76 per cent of the children with fathers employed in the professions (social class 1) attended some form of preschool group, whereas only 29 per cent of children of unskilled manual workers or the unemployed did so. In order to make their results more sensitive to children from one-parent families, Osborn and Milbank developed a composite social index comprising father's occupation, highest educational qualification of one (or only) parent, housing tenure, number of persons per room, type of housing, availability of a telephone, and possession of a car. Of those children rated as most disadvantaged (almost 10 per cent of the population), almost half had no preschool experience and, similarly, almost half of the disadvantaged children (20.4 per cent of the population), had not attended any type of nursery or play facility. By contrast, nine out of ten of the most advantaged (the 11 per cent who rated high on the composite social index) had experienced preschool group membership. Thus the social index uncovered even greater degrees of social inequality than the Registrar General's classification had done.

The educational priority areas set up in the 1960s and 1970s following the Plowden Report (CACE, 1967) included some projects which focused on preschool children. The idea that working–class children performed badly in school as a result of deprived home and family conditions led to 'compensatory' education. This style of working has been challenged by research studies by King (1978) and Sharp and Green (1975), who suggested that the effects of attending what amounted to middle–class schooling were really disenfranchising young working–class children. On the other hand, studies of working–class children at home by Davie *et al.* (1984) and Tizard and Hughes (1984) demonstrate that, far from being in linguistically and educationally impoverished homes, working–class children experience a rich and varied environment, but parents and children may be intimidated by teachers and schools, or view what they offer as irrelevant.

The emphasis on return for investment led, in any case, to an abandonment of these projects when it was thought that they were subject to a 'wash-out' effect, that is, that later academic test scores of children who had been involved did not continue to show their earlier promise.

Blackstone (1971) described the plight of children deprived of what she called a 'fair start'; she was later to assert (Blackstone, 1988) that positive discrimination, the practice of aiming provision at those most in need, should not have been declared a failure because it had never been properly attempted. Workers on the Home Link Project (Widlake, 1986) found to their dismay that they, like the families they worked with, were able to recognize faults in a system which were impeding change, but that recognition does not necessarily lead to change. In some cases it can lead to despair at one's powerlessness.

There have been many calls for change to an unfair system, among them the Court Report (Committee on Child Health Services, 1976) which stated that 'disadvantages of birth cast long shadows forward' (p. 3) and that 'educational failure should be recognised early ... many difficulties at school could be anticipated before school begins' (p. 11).

Conclusion

Longitudinal studies have indicated that the gulf in educational disadvantage or advantage between children widens inexorably as they move through primary school (see, for example, Douglas, 1964; Davie *et al.*, 1972). Becoming a university student may seem a far cry from being a preschooler, and there are no doubt some members of society who regard university experience as irrelevant. However, it remains one of the ways of gaining entry to a professional world and employment. It is therefore a useful measure of whether equality of opportunity is being achieved in Britain.

In 1983 women made up only 25 per cent of the undergraduate population; by 1987 this figure had risen to 44 per cent, and it is still rising. Whereas the postgraduate population was, in the past, largely male, there is now a high female proportion of research students, probably because male high flyers are being attracted into the City by the financial rewards they would relinquish in choosing academia.

Although there are no records available at the time of writing to indicate the position of black (Afro-Caribbean and Asian) ethnic minority students in relation to university entrance, CRE (1987) reported that only 2 per cent of teachers came from such groups. In 1986, out of seventy-five teacher training institutions replying to a questionnaire, only 2.5 per cent of graduates were black.

The career destinations of working-class children, as measured by university opportunities, are not encouraging. The chances of an advantaged teenager attending university are five times higher than those of a disadvantaged one. Despite the grant system (soon to be altered by the introduction of student loans) which may have been the reason why the UK record of working-class university entrance has not been as bad as that of France or the Netherlands (Little, 1986), the gulf does not seem to be narrowing. To say that there is no simple connection between class, gender, race and disability, is not the same as saying that connections do not exist – they do and they are complex. Once one has become sensitized to the effects of one of these as a disadvantaging condition, one is sensitized to the injustices perpetrated under the guise of differences which have been rationalized, through socially constructed categories.

It is not only the members of these groups who are missing out, as a result of discrimination and prejudice, since on the other side of the coin are the male, white, middle-class, 'normal' children who will grow up impoverished if they are left unable to empathize, and morally inadequate as a result of their own under-education.

As a white middle-class researcher in a black working-class preschool group, Sally Lubeck (1985) describes the painful disembedding of her prejudices and stereotypes, and her realization that the black women workers adopted certain teaching styles as a way of perpetuating group identity and solidarity. Their co-operativeness and cheerfulness in the face of adversity were survival strategies, comparable with the white middle-class workers' encouragement of competition, experimentation and manipulation. She concluded that to fulfil our most basic needs, to achieve, maintain, grow, belong and change, individually and together, we need to find ways of learning from each other.

8
An early years curriculum

We usually think of the word 'curriculum' in connection with schools, and, until fairly recently, many preschool practitioners were loath to admit that there was a curriculum in their establishments. For them, the idea of curriculum smacked of subjects, set lessons, and a syllabus, rather than their own view of what was important in the lives of young children – holistic development through free and spontaneous play.

Since the early 1970s, despite some lingering disagreements, educationists have not only clarified what may constitute the component parts of this concept we call 'curriculum', but have also considered the ways in which curricula are influenced by a variety of factors, such as our beliefs about childhood, our knowledge of child development, theories of child development, the political and economic conditions in the society in question, and the values and attitudes espoused by groups within that society.

For example, many people in the UK used to believe that two babies under a year old would in no way be capable of sharing objects or interacting. In Chinese and Russian nurseries babies would be deliberately allocated two to a cot with a single ball to share. The film *Infants at Work*, made by international nursery consultant Elinor Goldschmiel, shows such interactions between young British babies from the age of six months. The film suggests that one might use as a starting point a basket of carefully gathered 'treasures', objects which babies will love to explore for their smell, feel, appearance, sound and, in some cases, a lemon for example, taste.

As parents there are some learning experiences we set out to give our children, but we do not formulate our planned curriculum in the way that we would expect professionals to do. They are, after all, accountable to us as parents and to the rest of society for what our youngest citizens learn through contact with them. It is extremely important that all early years workers are able to articulate what children in their care enjoy and how and why they are subjected to particular experiences.

The Schools Council (1981) suggests that the curriculum is in fact 'what each child takes away with them', so that we need to examine the factors which will impinge on children, offering learning experiences through which they may internalize facts, skills, concepts and attitudes.

In this and the two following chapters I wish to explore what we call 'curriculum', looking at aims and objectives, teaching and learning styles, resources (such as space, equipment, and availability of adult contact), content, rules, use of the environment, assessment and evaluation, and relationships between staff and colleagues, staff and children, and staff and parents. I wish also to touch on those aspects of the curriculum we call 'hidden', factors not acknowledged consciously by the group or school. A school might, for example, praise excellence in maths but not acts of kindness. In some cases the relationships with parents, mentioned earlier, may not have been overtly acknowledged as part of the learning process and will therefore be part of the hidden curriculum. The hidden curriculum is an aspect to which I shall not address very much attention in this chapter, but it is important for teachers to realize its influence in the nursery, for if they do not attempt to make such factors conscious they will have no control over them. Most of us have probably been subjected to indoctrination, for example, in the areas of sexism and racism in particular, through the hidden curriculum we received as children.

During the mid-1970s the curriculum in primary schools became the subject of heated debate, because of disagreements among educationists and politicians over what was seen as 'valuable' education. Differing viewpoints arose out of ideological conflict. Alexander (1988) provides an analysis of some of the issues, describing seven ideologies, subscribed to by various protagonists in the debate about what education is for, and the resultant implications in respect of the curriculum (Table 1). As Alexander explains, although one ideology may be dominant at a particular time, the others do not cease to exist or to exert an influence, they are simply suppressed or in conflict with the one which is dominant.

What the arguments of the 1980s have brought about is the realization that children deserve, as a right, some kind of entitlement curriculum. The idea that decisions about the curriculum should be in the public, rather than narrowly educational domain, took root. Other countries had a national curriculum, with varying degrees of central control. British teachers were seen as wielding too much power and subsequent events led to the formulation of a National Curriculum (DES, 1987) for children

Table 1 Some dominant ideologies in primary education

Ideology	Central values in respect of curriculum
1 ELEMENTARY	Curriculum to meet society's economic and labour needs, and to preserve the existing social order. Education as a preparation for working life.
2 PROGRESSIVE	Curriculum to enable the child to realize his/her full potential as an autonomous individual. Childhood a unique phase of development, not just a preparation for adulthood. Curriculum open and negotiable.
3 DEVELOPMENTAL	Curriculum to be structured and sequenced in accordance with the child's psychological and physiological development and learning processes.
4 BEHAVIOURAL/ MECHANISTIC	Curriculum defined and structured in terms of hierarchies of observable and testable learning outcomes.
5 CLASSICAL HUMANIST	Curriculum about initiating the child into the 'best' of the cultural heritage, defined chiefly in terms of disciplines or forms of understanding: the arts, sciences and humanities.
6 SOCIAL IMPERATIVES: ADAPTIVE/ UTILITARIAN	Curriculum to meet society's economic, technological and labour needs, to enable the child to adapt to changes in these, and to preserve the existing social order.
7 SOCIAL IMPERATIVES: REFORMIST/ EGALITARIAN	Curriculum to enable the child both to fulfil individual potential and to contribute to societal progress. The latter defined in terms of plurality, democracy and social justice, as well as the economy.

Source: Alexander (1988, p. 157).

aged 5–16. Children aged five in September 1989 were the first of our youngest children to be subject to the new Education Reform Act, with its curriculum, in the form of courses of study (at present in the core subjects of maths, science and English) and their older infant/first school-mates will be the first to undertake the SATs, part of the profiling system which also includes teachers' continuous assessments.

For many people in the primary field there was anxiety that the construction of the National Curriculum had a secondary school orientation, being subject-based, according to the older view of the curriculum as comprised of disciplines. During the earlier part of the twentieth century, the rejection of a narrow, formal, basic subjects curriculum for young children was paralleled by the rejection of formal teaching methods. Blyth (1988, p. 13) suggests that it was Froebel, following in the footsteps of others such as Rousseau, whose focus on play as curriculum gave early childhood

> its own stake in curriculum...every age has a claim uniquely important to itself, as opposed to the established view that the most important learning must belong to the older pupils, who come nearest to the frontiers of human intellectual advance.

Some critics (e.g. Moyles, 1988) of the National Curriculum (DES, 1987) have stated, first, that young children need to learn in a cross-curricular fashion, to form links and to have learning reinforced through variety of experiences; and second, that the disciplines chosen were not always relevant for all children, or omitted important areas of experience, and certainly did not start from the child. The working groups who formulated the guidelines tried to allay some of these fears through their choice of content. It was made clear that those who taught through an integrated curriculum could continue to do so, and the Task Group on Assessment and Testing (DES, 1988c) put forward an assessment system which made the achievements of each child central, while emphasizing the importance of teachers' ability to match tasks to individual children's levels of achievement and experience.

Apart from those four-year-olds attending reception classes in primary schools who may be considered 'ready' to start on the National Curriculum, the early years field appeared to be untouched – but is it? Children are to be 'tested' at age seven, and the results used to grade schools, teachers and, of course, the children themselves according to those areas assessed. Given this, what of the discrepancies between not only early experiences at home, but also early experiences resulting from attending one preschool group rather than another, or from the length of time spent in preschool provision? Differences in preschool experience according to subcultural group have already been noted in Chapter 7. Will there be a 'top-down' effect on preschool provision, the child being subject to criteria dictated by later school requirements rather than by what is right for that child? What, in any case, will be the 'knock-on' effect on the preschool curriculum? Will different preschool curricula produce different effects, so that eventually a national preschool curriculum will be formulated? Is it reasonable to expect those who are not trained teachers, working in day nurseries, playgroups, or as nannies or childminders to formulate a curriculum? Do a variety of curricula already exist, though not all in a written statement? If so, what are the consequences for children of attending different institutions?

The early years curriculum

The construction of the preschool curriculum is said by Bruce (1987) to depend on the consideration of the child, the 'knowledge' chosen as relevant, and the environment (which includes significant people). She suggests it is the environment which is the means by which the child and the 'knowledge' are brought together. The skills, knowledge, concepts and attitudes to be acquired are embedded in the activities provided in the nursery.

Curtis (1986) points out the difficulties which have been experienced by those who have tried to formulate curricular aims for the nursery, that in fact there should be no difference in overall aims at any stage in the education process, and that what is perhaps most difficult is the formulation of behavioural objectives, that is, shorter-term and more narrowly defined goals for a particular group or child with a particular activity. What she suggests is that we examine what we offer in terms of whether or not it is 'worthwhile', quoting the educational philosophers Peters (1966) and Hirst (1969) who urged that worthwhile activities are those which are 'infinitely extendable', the process being more important than the product, and that we should be aware that some activities are 'inadequate for developing a body of concepts'. The excellent example Curtis (1986) gives of an activity where we should be asking ourselves just what we think children are learning that is worthwhile is that of sticking screwed-up tissue to teacher-prepared templates.

Commenting on the insistence in recent years that preschool curricula over-emphasize social and emotional development, Curtis (1986) argues that such criticism implies a lack of cognitive content in social or emotional episodes. Another criticism of those who would have early years practitioners devise neat and 'conveniently controlled programmes of instruction' comes from Blenkin and Kelly (1987). Their developmental curriculum is set in opposition to a 'traditional' curriculum which, they argue, over-emphasizes content – content, moreover, which has been selected as representing forms of knowledge enjoying 'mystical, God-given superiority'.

In contrast, the developmental curriculum is concerned to foster the 'maximum potential of every child to function as a human being ... with control over his or her own destiny' (p. 11); that decisions about content be made with reference to the child, with common developmental principles rather than common subject content; that education should proceed by learning *through* subjects, rather than *of* subjects; and that the greatest responsibility of educationists is to enable children to move from context-bound thought to 'disembedded' or context-free thought processes.

The developmental curriculum is sometimes confused with what was labelled 'progressive', and in some ways it is a curriculum built on that tradition, but with its roots firmly based on the findings of developmental psychologists. Such findings, critically assessed, inform the work of the early years practitioner in a way that was not always possible in earlier times, where progressives practised from a position of personal experience and belief, rather than acknowledging public evidence derived from research. This is not to denigrate personal experience. Thankfully, the most recent research studies take all these perspectives into account and acknowledge the fact that even rigorous, quantitative research can be problematic because of subjective bias in the selection of variables to be investigated, researcher effects, and so on.

The discrepant views about what constitutes a preschool curriculum, and reluctance on the part of some early years practitioners to delineate such a curriculum, arise as a result of the strongly held and traditional belief that the individuality of each child is central to early years provision (Bryans, 1987). This would mean that a child should be assisted in constructing his own curriculum. One might argue that, in pursuing their own interests, children can still be helped to develop skills, concepts, knowledge and attitudes, and that the crucial element will surely be sensitivity to the child's interests and appropriate provision of resources. Such sensitivity would, in Bryans's (1987) view, depend on three factors: providing for attachment to allow children to form a secure relationship with at least one worker; responsiveness from staff who ensure each child's learning and emotional needs are met; and familiarity in that there is continuity of experience in routine, location, grouping and adult contact.

From these examples, we can see that it is important for early years practitioners to be capable of articulating their views of the preschool curriculum. Generally speaking, they will begin from a consideration of the young child, his or her development, and the context in which he or she is developing. Since the early days of this century, and the women inspectors' report on under-fives in elementary schools (Bathurst, 1905), formal, subject-divided and teacher-directed schooling had been tried and found wanting as provision for the youngest children.

Unfortunately, as Alexander (1988; 1989) points out, the language which has been used most frequently in the past to discuss the early childhood curriculum has amounted to little more than slogans, such as 'play is a child's work' and 'children learn through play'. Smith (1986) has demonstrated that for some young children play does indeed amount to work, but in the sense that it is not freely chosen (one of the definitions of play), which calls into question the descriptions used by practitioners. Alexander is right – we do need to examine what we mean by the phrases we use. The cosiness of the past will no longer be allowed us, and if we wish to convice those who are making the decisions about what should be done in schools we must be capable of arguing clearly and cogently in defence of an early years curriculum which is built on that developed by the early pioneers – a curriculum based on children's interests and experience.

Play and the early years curriculum

Play is accepted as central to the curriculum of young children in modern, post-industrial societies. However, we saw in Chapter 5 that during the Industrial Revolution parents could be regarded as remiss in their responsibilities if they did not train their children for work, since there was little guarantee that the parent would be around for much of the child's life. It was through the work of such pioneers as Pestalozzi, Robert Owen, Froebel, Montessori (who valued constructive activities but considered fantasy play less important), McMillan and Isaacs, that play came to be viewed as the natural way to foster children's learning.

Children are observed to be highly motivated during play activities and play is believed to satisfy the conditions of a 'good' curriculum, since it may enable survival in customary surroundings; develop abilities which would later help career choice; be pleasurable; help children become members of society; foster the development of personal and moral qualities; act as a vehicle for the passing on of 'cultural' knowledge; and develop the ability to think and to use knowledge (Sutherland, 1988). This view of play as central in early childhood education was endorsed by the Plowden Report (CACE, 1967, para. 523): 'Adults who criticise teachers for allowing children to play are unaware that play is the principal means of learning in early childhood.'

Implicit in this philosophy is the view of the child as 'lone organism' (Bruner, 1984) rather than as social and cultural participant, and Piaget's theory has been used to legitimate the ensuing practice. The problem with the view that play is *the* mode of learning in the early years is that there are differences in interpretation about what this means in practice and, further, that workers often do not differentiate between different activities, all of which they label as play. This second point is extremely important because research on play indicates that some play does not lead to new learning.

Experimental psychologists have perhaps been less willing than practitioners to take beliefs about the benefits of play on trust. It may also be that during a recession we are likely to revert to our puritanical inheritance of pure fun being a sin, even for small children. This being the case, we need to justify play as a vehicle for learning, or at least to prove that it is useful for something. Researchers have investigated the possibility that certain play interests or styles of play may be the precursors of, say, creative thinking (e.g. Pepler and Rubin, 1982), which would, of course, be very useful in an entrepreneurial society.

Since play, especially fantasy play, is the antithesis of reality, could a curriculum based on play be under attack in this age of market forces and productivity? Sutton-Smith (1979) has suggested that societies use play as an early years curriculum to prepare children for life in a particular society and to foster conformity.

Nursery teachers who felt that they were fostering the way children developed through play opportunities may, in some cases, have been slow to accept the role of researchers in helping them justify their play-based curriculum, tease out which aspects of play prove beneficial, and develop improved practices. After all, some probably feared that 'improvement' might be seen in terms of values alien to those early childhood practitioners. Suppose, for example, it was suggested that better continuity of experience for children would result from greater teacher direction in order to prepare children for a possible or imagined repressive infant school regime in which children's initiative and independence were not valued and submissiveness and obedience were. Even nursery teachers, let alone other preschool workers, rarely enjoy equal status with teachers of older children, so it is natural for those engaged in the early years field to imagine that their views are the least likely to be heard and acknowledged. In the past, the rift between practitioners and researchers was due partly to lack of communication, partly to the committed nature of early childhood practitioners to the Plowden ideal (King, 1978) and partly to the (necessarily) open-minded view of the researchers, who believed they were behaving objectively and thus being true to science. Additionally, their methods were derived from ethologists who were studying animals. More recently, following the work of Stenhouse (1975) who fostered styles of research which many teachers find more appropriate to human beings, teachers and researchers are working collaboratively, with research likely to be either the work of the practitioners themselves, or carried out using methods involving practitioners, parents and children in comment upon what they, the researchers, are planning and observing. Since the central aim of all concerned is presumably the effective fostering of children's abilities, mutual trust and collaboration are vital.

Theories of child development offering support for learning through play

The work of Jean Piaget, mentioned earlier, has no doubt had the greatest influence so far on the early years curriculum in the UK. His

> insistence that knowing and thinking are active not passive ways of coping with the world is Piaget's first important contribution but Piaget under-emphasised... the role of apprenticeship to more knowledgeable others (including books and peers) in the construction of knowledge (Meadows, 1986, p. 34).

Piaget's theory of children's learning through interaction with the environment, assimilating (using already developed skills and concepts and incorporating items into existing schemata) and accommodating (adapting ideas and knowledge, making sense of what is being learned by adjusting to new knowledge), and the view that children are egocentric have become the underpinning of many early years curricula. Further, the idea that children must pass through certain stages in their development towards logical and abstract thinking, with the preschool stages being based very firmly on the senses and movement, has led some to interpret this into a nursery curriculum in which children have been left to explore materials or equipment without adult intervention, and their perceived needs as individuals have been the paramount concern of those working with them.

An alternative view, of the child as apprentice, as suggested by Vygotsky, whose work is only lately becoming well known in the West, places emphasis on social interaction in the development of cognitive abilities. Vygotsky also believed that the affective aspects of a learning situation should be taken into account, since the emotions can take over when a learner is overwhelmed by too much that is new. Vygotsky (1978) put forward the notion that the adult uses the 'ripening structures' of the child's learning and assists by offering support, focusing the child's next steps. He, too, supported the view that play should be the vehicle for such interactions.

This is similar to Bruner's (1977) view that the adult 'scaffolds' the child's experiences, whether these are play or non-play activities. Bruner (1984), who continues to make important contributions to the debate, discusses the fact that Vygotsky's work is perhaps a reflection of the Marxist society in which it was conceived, with its ideas of 'collective sharing' and 'transmission of new forms of consciousness across generations'.

Here in the West we were certain that by translating what we understood of Piagetian theory into practice (that is, by offering opportunities for learning through play), we were offering our children the best we could – lack of adult pressure, with children choosing activities for which they were 'ready', and active engagement, needed for assimilation and accommodation. What we may have done at the same time is encourage individualism.

Lubeck's (1985) study of two US preschool groups, one a white middle-class nursery and the other a black working-class Head Start nursery, shows how such differences in basic beliefs about how children learn, what they need to learn and why they need such curricula, influence the abilities of the children themselves. The individualism promoted in the white, middle-class children may be of value in some situations, but so is the co-operation and concern for others fostered in the black working-class group. In fact, both groups of children could benefit from the incorporation of the curriculum of the other.

Play and cognitive development

Arising out of his observations, Piaget's (1951) view of play and learning was a cautious one. He believed that children rehearsed skills and developed confidence in their growing abilities during play, so this was the assimilation phase of learning, but his evidence led him to conclude that certain constructive activities were of greater value for new learning, so that accommodation of the child's thought processes would take place. Despite Piaget's reservations, play came to be accepted as synonymous with learning, with rhetoric such as 'play is a child's work' being used as both justification and a way of developing solidarity among workers who had no really rigorous theoretical underpinning for their practice.

During the early 1970s a number of laboratory-based studies on play and cognitive development (such as Dansky and Silverman, 1973; Sylva, 1977) produced disappointing results, in that they provided neither clear evidence that play was the best mode for early childhood educators to adopt nor a rejection of play. The reasons for this are varied and perhaps complex – for instance, the short-term nature of the trials, the effects of the experimenters on the children and situation, the very fact that the situation was not the children's usual play setting, and so on.

Later, researchers began to use the methods developed by ethologists who studied the behaviour of animals, observing children in their customary nursery settings, mostly on a non-participant basis, like a 'fly on the wall'. Occasionally a researcher would set up or take part in particular activities and evaluate their effects. Some of these studies are referred to in this chapter.

First, observers began to ask what exactly we can classify as play. Are some of the behaviours we call 'play' really something else?' Hutt (1979), for example, rails against over-inclusiveness in what we categorize as play. For her, play is spontaneous, non-serious, unconstrained, pursued for its own sake, and, above all, fun. Although she agrees that in a colloquial sense we may call serious activity on the part of young children play, she suggests that when a baby, toddler or preschooler engages in concentrated investigation of an object or material it should be regarded as exploration. Hutt goes on to elaborate on the differences between play and exploration, indicating from her own research that children would first explore a new toy by approaching and inspecting it, then touching and manipulating. When the child seemed satisfied that she had learned the toy's properties, she appeared to move from the question of what the toy did, to the question of what she could do with it, at which point the activity became playful. The information the child had acquired during the exploratory phase was used in the play phase. Hutt had observed that behaviour during exploration was constrained, obligatory and systematically organized by every child, whereas play activity, the second phase, was more flexible, idiosyncratic and optional. Further, when sessions with the novel toy were offered at the rate of two per day, compared with sessions only every other day, children would play with the toy far less – that is, for play, familiarity seems to breed contempt – whereas exploration rates did not suffer this effect. Hutt suggests that the difference could be dependent upon the complexity of function and the child's level of cognitive functioning for exploration, whereas for play, factors like mood state, inventiveness and familiarity will influence interest. Parents who have been disappointed by their child's loss of interest in an expensive, but possibly limited, Christmas present in favour of the large carton in which the toy came will recognize this feature of children's behaviour!

In order to relate the activities of play and exploration to learning, Hutt (1979) suggests that during exploration children are acquiring knowledge and information – this is called 'epistemic' behaviour, while play behaviour is called 'ludic'. Hutt found that children cease to learn anything new during the ludic phase, they simply use information gathered during the epistemic phase. We can now see that the statement 'learning through play' is inexact. Furthermore, children will play only when their mood allows them to feel unconstrained. A child who is nervous or unhappy will not feel like having fun.

The value of both types of play is summed up by Tyler (1988, p. 5):

> there may be a balance to be struck between the two facets if the well-being of the child is to be nurtured. If a child exhibits an overwhelming preponderance of epistemic behaviour patterns, there is a danger that although learning is occurring, generalisation through the application of the skills and concepts is not. Similarly, if a child spends an undue proportion of his time engaged in essentially ludic forms of behaviour, there is a genuine danger that he may be missing out on situations in which the acquisition of fresh knowledge may occur.

Play with materials

Most nurseries provide play facilities like sand, water, clay and dough, paint collage materials, equipment for construction, mathematical, sequencing, writing and drawing activities, and so on, as well as small and large pieces of equipment to encourage fantasy and both gross and fine physical movement.

Some of the major research investigations into activities in preschool settings (such as Sylva *et al.*, 1980; Meadows and Cashdan, 1988; Hutt *et al.*, 1989) found that although most of the settings provided a rich environment, children's play was often desultory and brief. Sylva *et al.* (1980, p. 48) commented:

> If the child stands against the garden fence for ten minutes staring absently around him, they [teachers] claim he is learning by observing. If he repetitively puts dough into balls they say that 'the new baby at home is causing him to regress and he needs this simple act'.

There was little evidence of adult involvement in extending either conversation or thinking, and the free play curriculum in evidence in most of the settings did not offer enough cognitive challenge or indeed interactions with adults to provide the 'scaffolding' for new learning.

Staff in nurseries (Ward, 1982), especially the teachers, will claim that a range of potential benefits derives from different equipment. For example, they believe that water play fosters mathematical concepts. Yet the evidence from observations would lead us to believe (Hutt *et al.*, 1989) that much water play is repetitive and ludic. The missing ingredient here would appear to be the dialogue between children and adult, in which learning which has occurred during the exploratory phase becomes the focus of conversation and the teacher can provide whatever the children need to take their learning further, whether that be new or different equipment, questions and ideas, or help with planning an investigation. It is hardly surprising that parents think water play is provided for fun and socializing, and of course these are important aspects which teachers would wish to endorse, but it they think water play offers all the children in their group more than this they need to monitor, observe, take part in, evaluate and extend the activities at the water tray. The HMI (DES, 1989) report, which included consideration of nurseries, suggests that there are many nurseries where practice has been improved in this way, but is this true of all preschool establishments? It is possible that many are still unaware of Parry and Archer's (1974) distinction between 'two levels of play. One merely keeps children occupied; the other contributes to their educational development.'

Fantasy play

Interest in fantasy play, in particular the development of sociodramatic play tutoring, has been ongoing following the success reported by Smilansky (1968) with disadvantaged children in Israeli preschool groups. When children engage in role play, involving various assumed characters and events, they are taking part in one of the most complex forms of play (Smith, 1988). The view that pretend play should foster the ability to think in representational terms is supported by Vygotsky's (1978) theory, and Saltz and Brodie (1982) argue that Smilansky's research in the late 1960s led to research in play tutoring, since psychologists hypothesized that training children to participate in pretend play should foster language skills, problem-solving skills, divergent thinking and self-regulated, proactive behaviour, as opposed to behaviour elicited by external stimuli.

When children are left to engage in bouts of free fantasy play, these have been observed (Hutt *et al.*, 1989) yet again to entail only short activity spans, with few child–child social interactions and almost no adult engagement. This evidence confounds the widely held belief among early years practitioners that fantasy play fosters language development, along with socio-emotional development.

On the other hand, there is fairly strong evidence that fantasy play tutoring, either through adults offering the starting point of an outside visit, a thematic story or adult scaffolding by participation in the fantasy play, does afford cognitive benefits (Christie, 1986; Meadows and Cashdan, 1988; Hutt *et al.*, 1989). What is not yet clear is the actual reason for the cognitive gains, which may be due to factors other than the fantasy play tutoring *per se*. Possible factors resulting in the effect could be the adult scaffolding, the new experiences, and the forced engagement with materials which might otherwise be left unexplored but which become part of the fantasy.

In their report of observations carried out in their investigation of girls and mathematics, Walden and Walkerdine (1982) described and transcribed some of the fantasy play sessions of nursery children. What these passages show us are children manipulating both rules and symbolic objects and characters, children moving in and out of the fantasy as the mood and activity suited them. It seems important to acknowledge that such manipulation of ideas and symbols demonstrates considerable skills. But we must ask whether what we are observing during bouts of children-only fantasy play is useful for just that – observing what children we work with are rally capable of – or constitutes new learning taking place? Research seems to suggest (see for example, Smith and Sydall, 1978; Hutt, 1979) that when pretend play does result in cognitive gains, it is due to the language development resulting from the adult interactions. On the other hand, Smith (1986) wonders if the wrong outcomes of fantasy play may have been expected and measured, or the wrong procedures used in this research to date.

Language play

Although all aspects of language are available for use as play material, Kuczaj (1983) argues that there is a paucity of evidence on language play. Garvey (1977) discusses the ways in which infants will play with sounds and language in their cots early in the morning and before falling asleep at night. Many parents and teachers will be aware of the rhymes and nonsense language play of slightly older children, but most research studies concerned with language have discussed it mainly in terms of evidence of children's language development, adult–child interaction and the need for adult–child dialogue for the fostering of cognitive growth. Children are, at the nursery stage, beginning to be aware of the colloquial use of language. This is often language which confuses them at first. Laurie Lee's first day at school, described in *Cider with Rosie* Lee, (1959) is a marvellous example, with Lee wondering where his gift was when he was told to 'Wait there for the present'. When my older daughter was just three I remarked that I needed a haircut and wondered if the hairdresser could squeeze me in. She responded with a look of horror, and needed an explanation about her obvious misunderstanding.

Young children will sometimes find the sound of some words amusing and when they reach a stage of realizing *double entendres* this provides them with jokes – my younger daughter at just five became convulsed with bedtime giggles when she described the 'fluff' in her pillow as not being quite right, and realized the link with the cat, Fluff, in her school reading book.

Why is it that play with language is rarely used in school? Incongruity can often provide both fun and a challenge. Having young readers dictate a sentence to be written on paper, which can then be cut up into component words, can provide knowledge about what a sentence is, what a word is and endless practice, not to say fun, playing with the words of a pair of children together. For example, 'I like chocolate' and 'My Mummy is taking me to the shop' led to 'My Mummy is chocolate', among other gems.

Free play

The majority of the evidence appears to suggest that a preschool programme offering only free play with little or no adult involvement, the opposite end of the spectrum from a didactic, teacher-directed curriculum, will not ensure cognitive development. However, free play seems to be important for children's emotional development and it offers children opportunities to engage in social interactions with other children which are crucial learning experiences for life (Smith, 1986). Furthermore, during free play, especially fantasy play, children in a relaxed mood state will display a greater range of language ability than during their other activities, so that this makes it an important area for staff observation. Having observed the complexity of language and ideas used by children they had hitherto regarded as lacking in ability, or who were so often silent they were difficult to assess, may assist staff in matching their demands to children's needs.

A word of caution needs to be sounded, however. It would be easy to interpret the indication for greater adult involvement as a need for didactic instruction, or, as Smith (1986) suggests, 'work'. The way in which the adult intervenes will determine whether or not this happens. Staff in preschool settings where the 'stand back and light the blue touch-paper' approach still applies, despite their argument that they are pre-structuring the environment to encourage independent exploration and play, may need to help each other develop sensitive involvement in children's activities. Their role in scaffolding, in supporting children's learning, is reiterated again and again in research evidence and is discussed further in Chapter 10, and the HMI (DES, 1989) report gives some examples of how this is undertaken by skilled teachers.

> This view of the teacher as essentially a facilitator of learning was strongly emphasised by Vygotsky 50 years ago... As he put it, 'what the child can do today in cooperation, tomorrow he will be able to do alone'... The crucial word in that statement is cooperation... to be most effective the relationship between teacher and learner must, at every stage of development, be collaborative. Teaching thus seen, is not a didactic transmission of pre-formulated knowledge, but an attempt to negotiate shared meanings and understandings (Wells, 1985, p. 73).

It ain't what you do it's the way that you do it?

So far we have answered some of the questions set out at the beginning of this chapter on the preschool curriculum. We have research evidence which tells us that children learn certain things during free play, others in structured exploration, preferably with adult support, and that they need free play time as practice time and possibly also for rest and recuperation (Hutt *et al.*, 1989). The research evidence also seems to indicate that, in some preschool settings, children under five are indeed being under-educated because insufficient cognitive demands are being made of them and, generally speaking, it is the adult intervention which presents this challenge in dialogue.

A preschool curriculum which offers cognitive challenge, through both free and guided play and exploration, requires structure. Can research tell us what we should mean by 'structure'? Do differently structured curricula produce different outcomes?

In the early seventies David Weikart (Schweinhart *et al.*, 1986) compared three different American programmes. One was the early High/Scope curriculum based on the theories of Piaget; the second a more training- and task-oriented type of curriculum; the third a traditional free play nursery curriculum. The outcome of his research, in terms of the gains made by the children from the three programmes, was that the programme itself did not matter as much as other factors. These factors were a consistent daily routine; commitment by staff to the aims of the nursery curriculum; efficiency in planning the work of the nursery; and systematic and applied evaluation of what had happened. In other words, the conclusion was it ain't what you do it's the way that you do it. Although admitting that firm conclusions should not be drawn from their small sample, the Weikart team suggest that their follow-up studies indicate that long-term effects are dependent upon the early experiences in preschool programmes in which attention is paid to the quality of the adult–child relationships, to curriculum coherence and to pupil initiation of activities.

In a similar vein, Jowett and Sylva (1986) asked 'Does kind of preschool matter?' They followed ninety children from preschool through their first six months in reception class at primary school. Half the group had attended a playgroup, half a nursery class, and all were from working-class homes. Their results were in line with Weikart's (Schweinhart and Weikart, 1980) second American study, in which this time the High/Scope programme produced children who were more committed to school and able to work on a task than children who had not attended a preschool group. Jowett and Sylva's study indicated that the room organization, availability of resources, and higher level of interaction with adults experienced by the nursery class children, compared with the limitations due to space, time, money and learning opportunities in playgroups, led to the nursery children appearing better able to cope with the demands of life in the primary school, being more independent, showing greater complexity in play, longer concentration spans and being more likely to approach the teacher as a resource for learning than simply for help.

A long-term study of children in North London by Dye (1984) indicated that children in an experimental nursery group, who were offered a curriculum based on Curtis and Hill's (1978) *My World*, made gains in a variety of areas in comparison with the control group which experienced a traditional, free play nursery curriculum. Furthermore, some of the gains persisted over the infant school years. This is one of few studies which have examined the influence of different preschool curricula on social competence, and Dye states that those involved were surprised to discover that the experimental group became more mature socially than the controls. Could this be due to a number of factors, for example, the expectations of the staff, the increased demands on children generally and, again, the fact that there was probably more adult–child and child–child dialogue in focusing on the required tasks?

One curriculum which has received considerable press coverage, and which is gaining in popularity in Britain, is the High/Scope curriculum mentioned above. Some believe it is a curriculum which originated with people like Susan Isaacs, and while British nurseries interpreted Piaget's work as meaning free play, this cognitively oriented curriculum crossed the Atlantic. As part of the Head Start programme of compensatory education initiated in the 1960s, David Weikart and his colleagues (Weikart *et al.*, 1971) devised a preschool curriculum based on the theory that children construct their own knowledge through activity which results in learning. The High/Scope programme involves a well-planned nursery layout; the staff engage with children in helping them plan their own activities, gather the necessary resources, monitor the children's efforts, recording what has been experienced, and finally help the children review what they have done. The staff record each child's activity in terms of lists of 'key experiences', which are not regarded as goals in themselves but as essential elements to be experienced repeatedly, 'like vitamins and other nutrients'. The key experiences provide a structure for staff to evaluate each child's curriculum, as well as the opportunities they are able to offer in their nursery. At each session children will engage in the process of 'plan, do, review' and the goals of the curriculum are to foster children's ability to make choices; use time and energy efficiently; develop self-discipline; and pursue self-chosen tasks; work with others; develop skills in the arts, physical movement and knowledge of objects; develop abilities to communicate and to express ideas and feelings, to understand others, and apply reasoning abilities; and develop children's initiative, spirit of inquiry, open-mindedness and ability to empathize.

An independent evaluative research study by a team based at Oxford University covered the effects of British High/Scope training and implementation between 1984 and 1986. In their final report (Sylva *et al.*, 1986) the team suggest that with experience, staff adapt the curriculum to suit their needs and that it provides a useful tool for evaluation and planning. Children attending High/Scope nurseries are said to become more independent learners, spending less time 'aimlessly' wandering around, disrupting others or waiting to be directed by adults and more time thinking for themselves. Critics of the approach argue that it offers less scope for the involvement of parents than is suggested by the literature, that the doctrinaire aspects of the High/Scope movement are likely to close staff minds rather than opening them to a range of possibilities, especially in the sense that focusing on children's self-chosen materials from what is available within a nursery leads to a limiting of opportunities by not involving the wider environment. Inexperienced staff are reported to respond to the demands of the High/Scope methods by spending their days rushing round with checklists simply monitoring what children are doing rather than engaging in conversation with them, and fail to foster co-operative ways of working, so that the children tend to work individually. Others will argue that it is difficult for children to make choices until they have some experience of what is possible. In free play nurseries many 'new' children will behave like butterflies, tasting many activities briefly until they are reassured that there will constantly be chances to paint, to explore the water tray, the construction equipment or the dressing-up clothes. The results of the observational study (Hutt *et al.*, 1989) of children attending conventional nurseries does indeed show that children spend approximately a third of their time walking or running around, looking around or watching others. This was true of all types of preschool group studied and irrespective of whether the children were indoors or out. For children new to the group the proportions were higher than for more experienced attenders. As one would expect, children who had established themselves and knew the opportunities, the daily routine, the adults and other children, would spend a greater proportion of time engaged in activities. If this is not so for children in a High/Scope programme, and we have no evidence as yet of differences in time on task and so on, does it mean that the conventional nursery is allowing too long for children to 'waste time' and therefore miss out on learning experiences, or does it mean the High/Scope children are missing out on the opportunity to 'stand and stare'?

Perhaps the most important issue in any curriculum development is the need for all members of staff to engage in discussion about their underpinning philosophy – what they believe early childhood education is for, how children learn and develop, what their own and parents' roles should be and implications for practice. Any curriculum development arising from an outside agency, whether it is the LEA, the government or another body (in the case of High/Scope this was VOLCUF), will take time to adapt to the needs in individual institutions, and initial training, if needed, should be undertaken by at least two members of staff who can support each other, since one alone, even if it is the Head, can be isolated. In fact, where it is the Head who participates in outside training, other staff may simply comply because of the imbalance of power, however good the relationships. In most cases, such curriculum development would not be sustained after that Head leaves the group because other staff would not have been sufficiently committed to the initial changes.

Comparisons between curricula lead us back to our earlier question about what is meant by the word 'structure'. Moore and Smith (1987, p. 13) state that 'it is a contentious issue in British preschool provision and not an easy term to define'. But since Alexander (1988) accuses practitioners of obfuscation through the use of slogans and thus hegemony (guarding of power), it is essential that we employ less emotive language and recognize the fact that flexibility and structure need to be explained rationally. High/Scope professionals feel that because the structure of the day, the layout of the nursery and the pattern of activities expected of children is known by those children, the structure is 'invisible' (Sylva *et al.*, 1986) yet provides a framework for staff discussion.

Whether High/Scope or not, in a nursery which adopts this type of invisible or transparent structure, its presence felt more than seen, staff, together with parents, will discuss planning room layout, the purpose of activities, use of children's and adults' time, adult roles, observation and assessment, and so on.

According to Woodhead (1976) and Hutt *et al.* (1989), a nursery in which everything is implicit, unplanned and not discussed makes overwhelming demands on the children to understand and take advantage of what is offered and, similarly, heavy demands on individual staff to ensure maximum benefits for each individual. Such loose organization is also open to misuse and can be as insidious as an overly opaque or rigid structure which does not allow children opportunities to develop autonomy.

It is interesting that the High/Scope curriculum is seen as roughly central on a continuum ranging from *laissez-faire* to adult-directed. In a *laissez-faire* nursery regime, the equipment is usually put out by staff and children are then left to play, as described earlier. The implicit pre-structuring of the environment in this way could in fact be more limiting than one in which no equipment is put out and children choose from what they know.

An exciting adaptation of the High/Scope curriculum currently being established in some early years classes is that of providing children with 'starting points'. The starting point may be the local shop, or a basket of various fruits, and children choose the activities they wish to pursue after consideration and conversation. The type of planning required for such curriculum development involves discussion of adult roles, planning potential requirements for child-chosen activity, collection of resources and decisions about records and assessment. It will also raise the issue of how time should be spent, should part of each session be left for free play, how children can be encouraged to work in pairs, or in a group, and so on.

The skills needed by the adults working with young children are discussed further in Chapter 10 but it is important to add here that research shows that teachers vary in how much they plan and their resultant effectiveness. Alexander (1988), whose study concerns teachers of older primary school children, describes the differences in planning depending upon experience and, especially, confidence in personal ability in particular curricular areas. A mathematician is, quite logically, more likely to be able to seize upon the mathematical aspects of a cross-curricular theme, evident in children's chosen activity, than a non-mathematician. Non-specialists may be prone to missing such opportunities unless they plan and there is a danger that unless the planning involves a specialist the result could be a more didactic approach than one would wish. Davie *et al.* (1984) found that parents were often unaware of informal learning opportunities and would resort to teaching from special books and so on as a result. The expertise brought to cross-curricular work by specialists with that sensitivity to naturally occurring learning opportunities is equally important in the preschool field. A mathematician, for example, may capitalize on children's fascination, for example, with the number, shape, size and pattern of segments in oranges they are preparing for a snack, or the beauty of the symmetry in the pattern revealed when an apple is cut across its 'equator'.

Metacognition – learning to learn

Although the work of Holt (1969), many years ago, drew attention to the idea, it is only during the 1980s that psychologists have begun to question whether awareness of one's own thought processes, knowing what one does and does not know, a process called *metacognition*, results in differences in cognitive ability.

Nisbet and Shucksmith (1986) suggest that even very young children have a considerable amount of knowledge about their own cognitive processes but that they do not use this insight when faced with a task. Some of the early research studies claimed to demonstrate that possession of metacognitive knowledge made no difference to performance and was therefore probably irrelevant. However, Brown's (1977) work showed that children's metacognitive skills do indeed develop faster than their ability to use this knowledge spontaneously, and further research indicates that the style adopted by parents serves as a modelling device for young children (Beveridge and Dunn, 1980; Light, 1979; Robinson and Robinson, 1982).

When asked to clarify ambiguous statements, to explain what they meant, children were provided with regulation, or scaffolding, to their language and thought processes, by parents who later removed that scaffolding when the child became competent at self-regulation.

This ability to reflect and examine what one means is important, yet it appears that in most school situations we do not enable even those children who have developed the ability to use it, and, perhaps more crucially, we do not foster it in children who appear to lack the necessary skills. Edwards and Mercer (1987) found that while teachers in primary schools believed that children should learn through direct experience, they were covertly developing in children a dependence upon them because they did not relinquish control – the children were never ready for the scaffolding to be removed. One of the factors contributing to this problem was the way in which dialogue was rooted in the classroom activities, rarely transcending the boundaries of the concrete, the here and now, and becoming disembedded. Awareness of general principles and awareness of one's own thought processes are rare occurrences and their relative absence from life in school or nursery is something we should address, for it may be that there simply is not enough time to engage in conversations which do develop these abilities. The way in which children in the High/Scope programme are required to plan and review their chosen tasks could be a route to such dialogue with children.

Perhaps we need to evaluate our preschool curricula and ask ourselves not simply about children, curriculum as knowledge, skills, concepts and attitudes, and the translation of curricular aims into practice, but also why this curriculum rather than another. We are told that John Stuart Mill could not remember ever being allowed to play (we cannot rule out the possibility that he repressed his memories of play because of his father's attitude, of course) so is play really necessary? In her study of the role and status of play, Moyles (1989) gives ample justification for encouraging and valuing play in early childhood education, though she, too, points out that 'children can and do learn in other ways than through play, and often enjoy doing so. An example would be in listening to a story or working alongside adults making or achieving something' (Moyles, 1989, p. 24). This does raise a serious question about how much of a preschool curriculum should be *real* activity and how much play in which we would not engage were no children present. *Real* activity is indeed attractive to young children, they enjoy making bread to share with others, feeding the guinea pig, sharing in shopping and so on. It is when we exclude them or show that we find their 'help' a hindrance that they turn off and go to 'play'. I am not advocating that we do away with toys, or that we expect children to work in the productive, old-fashioned sense. But could the curriculum offered include activities through which young children feel more valuable as contributing members of the society in which they live?

9
Assessing children's progress

During the 1980s the assessment of children under five in nursery schools and classes, and the recording of their progress, has come to be seen as an essential element of good practice. This does not always appear to have been the case.

Developing assessment

Although Isaacs (1929) encouraged the careful observation of children, a post-war survey (Walker, 1955) indicates that, unless records were kept internally, the practice of assessment and recording was virtually non-existent until the late 1970s. Many practitioners will be able to remember the reasons why assessment and the keeping of records were considered inappropriate at this stage. First, group or class planning in too detailed a manner was discouraged, since it was thought that this would impose too much rigidity, rather than encouraging staff to allow for spontaneous events developed out of children's own suggestions. Apart from the constraints imposed by organization relating to mealtimes and a daily or sessional story and singing period, usually at the end of the session, the day was not 'timetabled'. Certain planning, relating to which equipment would be offered at each session, meant that there was a degree of pre-structuring of the environment, but little would be predetermined within that time-slot, other than perhaps such matters as which member of staff would be on duty in the toilets for the pre-lunch preparations. There was little discussion of why certain activities were to be presented, and who would undertake which adult task. In most cases it was as if meanings, purposes and roles were part of a shared understanding.

This 'crisis management' style is amply reported by Clift et al. (1980).

Individual records of children's activities and progress were discouraged for fear of labelling, and in any case, primary school staff paid little heed to the offerings of nursery staff, possibly due to a difference in ethos or emphasis, so it is not surprising that nursery teachers were reluctant to spend time completing records for transition purposes. The idea of offering parents a detailed assessment of what their child was capable of was strangely lacking, too, almost as though there was a divide, with the nursery seen as a private world for the child, one in which parents should respect the child's rights to a life separate from them. Any shortcomings, therefore (for assessments at this time would be likely to be negative), would be regarded as the secret domain of staff, only divulged to parents if the child became the focus of attention through a desperate need for official diagnosis or help from a professional outside the nursery team.

Assessment in the early years, other than that relating to physical disabilities, was generally viewed as relevant if it pertained to reading, writing and mathematics, very often the only areas of progress on which first schools kept formal records, and nursery staff would take care not to impinge on these, since such aspects of the curriculum were seen as the domain of the infant teachers.

This account highlights the main factors regarded as important reasons for keeping records of assessment of children – or not. Unless a child was perceived to have some sort of difficulty, in which case the appropriate (other) professional was called in, there was thought to be no reason to assess children or to keep records, other than those detailing aspects of children's development made possible by nursery school medical examinations.

What staff were not taking into account, however, was the fact that they were often making judgements about children and the activities in which they engaged. These were, after all, assessments, but they were assessments which were largely unacknowledged by the staff themselves or by others. The value of what could be called 'intuitive', spur-of-the-moment judgements was not recognized, nor the reflection, awareness and experience which one needed to perform such assessments well and as objectively as possible. Bennett and Kell (1989) suggest that while early years teachers are generally good at such assessment, they do not follow this with diagnosis, so that appropriate learning activities will be presented to the child as the next step.

Towards the end of the 1970s, partly as a result of a number of the research projects which had been carried out in Europe and the United States and partly as a response to demand for greater accountability by all teachers, there was growing acceptance among nursery head teachers that some record keeping was useful and, far from impeding spontaneity, could actually enable the teacher to match resource provision and task demands to individual children's needs. Further, it could enable staff to work in greater communion because all would understand the purposes of different activities and thus develop team management in order to free particular members of staff to carry out more prolonged observation or intervention work with children in the group.

As psychologists became sensitive to the need for criterion-referenced assessment (recording what children can do so that help with the next steps is possible), rather than norm-referenced material (judging children's performance against the scores of a large population of children of the same chronological age) (see Lunt, 1983), so materials began to be developed to assist nursery teachers. Psychologists realized that telling staff a child's IQ score is of little help in solving the child's difficulties, or rather, the teacher's difficulties in knowing how best to foster that child's learning. The best way to help all concerned - child, parent and teacher – was for all to work together, with the support of the psychologist.

Some tests are still the preserve of educational and clinical psychologists, for particular diagnoses (for example, Griffiths Mental Development Scales), and others, such as hearing or sight tests, will be carried out by appropriate members of other professions. The early education professional, however, is often the person who first suspects and monitors for evidence of, say, a hearing loss. If a child is inattentive during story sessions, is it because of the child's inexperience, age, boredom or inability to make sense of something that is, to that child, inaudible and incomprehensible?

The advent of the *Keele Preschool Assessment Guide* (*KPAG*) (Tyler, 1979) and the NFER Manual (Bate *et al.*, 1978), gave greater emphasis to the gradually occurring landslide of interest in evaluating and recording in nursery education. Nursery staff became even more conscious of the need to carry out continuous assessment of children's abilities, in order to enable their development through what staff, mainly teachers (Moore and Sylva, 1984), diagnosed as the individual child's next stage. During this period the survey of primary schools by HMI (DES, 1978a) had drawn attention to the need for teachers to 'match' tasks to children's abilities, and nursery staff, ever in the vanguard of those who subscribed to the Plowden ideology of the child as central and as starting point of the education process, took these helpful assessment tools to heart. It was also during this time that the post-Piagetians, for example Donaldson (1982), Hughes (1978) and McGarrigle and Donaldson (1974), carried out work to further the insights given us by Piaget's own work. What they helped practitioners realize was the importance of context, helping children make sense of new cognitive challenges by presenting them in a familiar or relevant guise, and of using familiar language. Prior to this work practitioners had been led to rely too heavily on the notion that children's cognitive development progressed according to the stages set down in Piaget's theory and that these were immutable.

Moore and Sylva (1984) discovered that more than half of the 125 local authorities sampled in their study had some form of standard records and the most popular reasons for keeping records of assessments made in the nursery were those relating to planning whole-team and individual children's activities. Many of these assessment and recording systems were based on one of the published schemes mentioned above, the *KPAG* and the NFER Manual. The *KPAG* was proposed as a stimulus to schools in developing their own assessment or profiling systems, whereas the NFER Manual discouraged such adaptation as invalidating the pack. The importance of staff involvement in developing assessment methods suiting their contextual needs, together with the shorter original format of the *KPAG*, may have been contributory factors in its greater popularity (Moore and Sylva, 1984).

Its author, Stephen Tyler, is currently working with groups of nursery teachers in the North-West of England on an update of the *KPAG*, particularly in the areas of problem-solving skills and assessment of bilingual children. The types of assessment in these packs are strongly focused on the observed behaviour of the child being assessed, with staff being encouraged to see such observation as the only objective way of assessing children's abilities. Some teachers might also wish to encourage children to talk about their achievements, so as to learn more about individual children, at the same time fostering the children's ability to be reflective.

The local authorities where staff were beginning to use such methods of assessment and recording were also likely to be those in which they were asked to ensure they evaluated the work of their teams (see City of Sheffield, 1986).

Evaluation of work in a nursery is an essential part of team planning. It is during evaluation sessions that teams can discuss items on record sheets, so as to avoid the impression that chosen behaviours are regarded as sacrosanct, checklists as 'tablets of stone'. Periodic reviews of what a team (and this will include parents, governors and advisers) values in terms of items to be recorded as children's achievements are vital. In the same way, the National Curriculum and attainment targets must be viewed as a rather ambitious experiment, to be adjusted in the light of experience.

This enmeshing of evaluation of provision with the assessment of the children in the nursery is an important feature of these developments.

The monitoring of the relationships between the planned curriculum, the curriculum offered in practice, and that experienced by individual children led teachers to understand that they needed to develop skills of observation, evaluation and planning, requiring time and a degree of awareness which in itself demanded time to acquire. One of the constraints operating in most nursery situations is that unless staff are willing and able to spend time outside the sessions on this type of in-service development, there is no free slot during the day when all staff can come together. (Some must be with the children throughout, since meals supervisors are not generally provided for nurseries.) Teachers may have contracts in which demands relating to non-contact hours are made, but other workers, nursery nurses and ancillaries, for example, may feel that their conditions of service, particularly their low pay, do not encourage them to spend their own time on this, despite their overall commitment to their work. Additionally, although there are courses in some areas for day nursery staff, playgroup personnel, childminders, and others not regarded as specifically educational early years workers, there are similar constraints, such as lack of funding, lack of time, and lack of awareness in their work context of the existence of a 'curriculum' and of any associated assessment.

As stated above, such workers are very likely to be making informal judgements about individual children but are these assessments more often focused on the perceived main concern of their institution? In the playgroup, for example, are the informal judgements concerned with children's friendships, ability to stay without a parent, and so on? In the day nursery, are they concerned with children's aggression, or disruptive behaviour, or signs of emotional disturbance, rather than with an overall view of the child and evaluation of their own actions and provision to help the children cope with learning in spite of family difficulties?

What we need to ask in terms of the deal under-fives are currently getting is whether such monitoring is of value. If so, do all under-fives in nurseries and primary schools experience such monitoring? Are children in non-education establishments likely to be monitored in a similar way?

How does this process fit in with the National Curriculum and assessment the children will experience once they enter primary school? Do we want a national assessment system for all children under five?

Is the assessment of children under five of any value?

There have so far been no evaluations of the long-term use of assessment procedures in preschool establishments. Where such practices have been monitored, such as in the screening of children diagnosed as having special educational needs, there is a dilemma in interpreting later educational progress as reflecting a beneficial effect of screening by early testing, since the children involved could have developed perfectly well without the provision which resulted.

Qualitatively, the kinds of benefits reported by staff regarding the use of assessment and recording procedures include awareness among the staff team of aims and objectives, purposes of activities, better team organization and planning, and preparedness for the needs of individual children. This preparedness is particularly important in the sense that staff who have observed children for the recording of the children's abilities can intervene in play situations where the children themselves are making the choices and decisions, and foster each child's activity at an appropriate level, without the intervention becoming overly didactic. Moore and Sylva (1984) report nursery staff as stating that they kept records primarily for team planning and for planning for individual children's learning needs.

In contrast, infant teachers reported that they kept records in order to pass on information to the next teacher or school. The fact that transition records receive scant attention from teachers in a subsequent stage (DES, 1978a) has been part of a move towards greater agreement about what kinds of records should be passed on. Indeed, some schools have begun to experiment with the idea of children keeping their own profile folders, to which they and their parents, and presumably any other interested parties – for example, a dance or gym coach – could contribute as well as staff in school.

It could be argued that indirect evidence of the value of continuous assessment and a carefully thought-out recording system is implicit in the work of the High/Scope programmes from the USA. Berruetta-Clement *et al.* (1984) argue that long-term benefits accrue from preschool programmes based on a developmental model. Such a programme would involve monitoring children's activities and reviewing progress.

Do all under fives experience this monitoring process?

It is possible that, since Moore and Sylva (1984) found that just under half their sample recorded children's progress, the remainder of the local authorities have implemented a system of assessment for children in nursery schools and classes. It is also possible that some have not. Further, HMI reports detail the ways in which the curriculum, of which such assessment procedures would be an element, is not fully developed in all groups currently visited by them.

In their report following a comprehensive survey including 300 visits, made between 1985 and 1988, across the range of preschool educational provision, HMI (DES, 1989, p. 9) state the view that:

> in the best circumstances, the teaching is informed by a careful assessment of the overall programme and the response of each child to the learning activities which are provided. Judgements about the children's learning are recorded so that their progress can be planned and monitored over time.

Establishments without any teacher input will presumably be more likely to await some guidance on this matter, and, in the case of playgroups and childminders or nannies, it seems very unlikely that such assessment and recording will be seen as part of the worker's role in any formal sense, though individual workers may be meticulous about drawing the attention of parents to particular problems.

It is not my intention here to discuss how staff may make assessments through observing children engaged in exploration and play activities (see, for example, David and Lewis, 1989, Campbell *et al.*, 1990), but to examine the issues arising out of assessments of children under five.

Will the assessments related to the National Curriculum in schools have any effect on preschool children?

There are fears that many problems will arise as a result of assessment in primary schools relating to the National Curriculum. These fears tend to revolve around the early statementing of children who are expected to fare badly on the assessments and downgrade the school's overall score. By statementing potentially low achievers, who will then be labelled, the school may, for a time, gain the exemption of these children from the National Curriculum and possibly also from the aggregated levels of attainment of the school.

Another group for whom early years workers must have concern in relation to standard tests at seven are children from minority groups for whom English is not the mother-tongue. Although bilingual SATs are being developed, how will these be administered, and what are the implications of the context in which the tests are embedded?

Children who have had little preschool experience, at least of the type they capitalize on after entering school, may also be discouraged from admission to certain schools, or when admitted, meet with undue pressure to 'catch up'. At the 1989 Annual Conference of the AMMA (TES, 1989) a resolution was tabled advising heads to 'test' children on entry to primary school in order to assess progress made during the infant years. If head teachers are intending to test children at four, how will they carry out such tests in areas where, for example, their bilingual support is either non-existent or sporadic, and if children are tested at four, how valid will such tests be, particularly for children to whom the school is a strange and alien environment?

Pre-entry or base-line assessments can be viewed in a number of ways. First, they might be a device to protect the teaching staff of schools in areas where children are expected to do less well on the national SATs to be set at seven, than those children in more advantaged areas. Is there a danger that staff in such schools are finding excuses for themselves, or do they have a right to expect *progress* (rather than level of achievement at seven) to be the measure of their effectiveness? Furthermore, will children be labelled by the on-entry assessments, or will the assessments be used to prevent failure, to give help where it is needed, as Tizard (see TES, 1988b) and Desforges (1989) suggest? The third point is highlighted by the ongoing debate between these two researchers in the pages of the *Times Educational Supplement* in the spring of 1989: should assessments carried out to prevent later under-achievement be intuitive continuous assessments by the teacher or bought-in standardized formal tests with high test-retest reliability? There are issues to be considered in relation to both. If the tests used have a high test-retest reliability, are the tests any practical use, since the very nature of doing the testing is in order to prevent the retest producing the same result. This effect could simply lead a teacher to test and assume she may as well concentrate on those children who will achieve high scores, since there is apparently nothing she can do to help the under-achievers in the long run. On the other hand, Crocker and Cheeseman's (1988) study shows the way in which young children very quickly adopt the 'pecking order' ascribed by the reception class teacher, who has categorized her class through intuitive assessments. As Desforges (1989) suggests, what is required is a way of developing the skills and awareness of teachers in the judgements they make.

Part of the debate when formulating such an assessment schedule must be centred upon the criteria chosen as evidence of an achievement. How will the chosen assessment items be related to the later profile components, and will this early assessment be broader than that required for the National Curriculum and in line with current good nursery practice?

The advantages of the system which has been devised for assessment (DES, 1988c) are in fact of a type which could benefit nursery education in one sense. Although the National Curriculum itself has been criticized for its division by subject, the style of assessments to be carried out at seven and 11 is likely to encourage cross-curricular work and there is no prescription about how the curriculum is to be taught. Work by a group based on the NCB (1987) has culminated in a publication concerning the early years curriculum from three to seven; as Lally (1989) points out, there should be continuity for the children and, as with the implementation of the National Curriculum for every age-group, staff must have the confidence to begin from their own good practice and examine the ways in which the programmes of study and the attainment targets of the National Curriculum fit into their practice, rather than the other way round. If one begins by examining the ways in which structured play fosters children's physical, social, emotional and cognitive development (and I am including moral, spiritual, scientific, technological and aesthetic development in these headings), the emerging skills form the basis for later learning. These skills include investigational skills, such as questioning and guessing; the development of concepts, for example mathematical concepts like height, and scientific concepts such as living/ non-living; together with acquiring knowledge (facts); and positive attitudes about themselves, their classmates and their learning experiences. The greatest danger to a broad and balanced early years curriculum in which there is progression and differentiation appropriate to each child's needs will be from lack of teacher confidence and a resulting teacher-directed 'teaching to the tests'.

According to HMI (DES, 1989), the curriculum in nursery schools is more appropriate for children under five than the curriculum in primary schools. Bennett and Kell (1989) found in their study that children in reception classes were subjected to a narrow curriculum based on the three Rs like that HMI reported in its surveys of primary and first schools (DES, 1978a; 1982). Their findings are similar, too, to those reported at the SCDC/NFER Conference (see Bennett, 1987; Sestini, 1987; and Stevenson, 1987) with four-year-olds slaving over narrow 'work', and play activities regarded as very second-rate (taking up only 6 per cent of the children's time in the classes observed for Bennett and Kell's study).

The interconnections between learning activities and assessments as component parts of the curriculum mean that teachers need to examine very carefully what it is they think children are learning from what happens in their classrooms. If teachers with four-year-olds in primary classes are unable to recognize the value of play, or perhaps lack the confidence to implement a programme of structured play, they are also likely to be unable to understand how to carry out assessments through observing and participating in children's play. As Clark (1983) pointed out teachers of reception class children may make glib assumptions based on their knowledge of whether or not a child has experienced some form of preschool provision, or on what form that took, and believe that the child's failure with her is the result of the earlier provision, not the result of her inappropriate teaching strategies and her own failure to relate to the skills the child does possess.

Although many teachers and parents believe that earlier entry to primary school will mean higher academic achievements later, this is not borne out by research evidence from the UK or the USA (Osborn and Milbank, 1987; Zigler, 1987). Furthermore, in primary schools where the head teacher and parents do not understand how children learn through experimentation and exploration in play situations, there is probably immense pressure on the reception class teacher to conform to their view. The private sector, currently increasing in popularity and expanding its preschool provision, is even more subject to the wishes of parents, since they are paying directly for the school's services, and it seems likely that four-year-olds in this form of provision will have less time for play than any other group, with the work-play divide very clearly marked, and play regarded as a waste of time.

Again, a potential danger of the SATs at seven could be their use as a moderating device taking precedence over the ongoing assessments made by class teachers. Like nursery teachers, reception and other infant class teachers generally have low status and have learned to adopt this opinion of themselves. The fact that the implementation of the National Curriculum officially begins in autumn 1989 with classes of five-year-olds may help alter this view. Although there will be no SATs (DES, 1988c) for the five-year-olds, and thus no official moderating groups, the positive benefits of being first to begin work officially on the National Curriculum may mean that moderation or support groups both within and between schools may be set up to offer teachers opportunities to discuss process and product and ways of assessing progress. This may counterbalance the gradual demise of the nursery infant and first schools, through their reincorporation into primary schools – usually with a junior-trained teacher as head – which has often resulted in the colonization of the infant classes. Top-down pressure to teach in the way that junior classes have usually been taught, often as a result of further top-down pressure from the secondary schools, has been more difficult to resist than it was when early years teachers were in separate schools. The National Curriculum could therefore have a positive effect on the learning opportunities of our youngest primary school children, linking well within nursery experience.

Do we want a national curriculum and assessment system for children under five?

Lloyd (1983) argued that if we are so certain that children benefit in the long term from preschool provision, why do we not lobby for the school entry age to be compulsorily reduced to three in place of five?

This idea is probably anathema to most people in the UK especially those who work in the field of early years education and care. If it is a culturally determined response, which seems likely, it is also a probable response to the idea of universal assessment of children under five. But do we respond in the same way when we are considering health assessments? We expect our children to be screened and given the support or treatment they need in order to ensure that any condition discovered by such screening has a minimal effect in the long term. Why are we squeamish about a similar system in relation to learning needs?

Perhaps our greatest feelings of antipathy towards the idea of assessments of young children comes from our fear of early labelling, and it is often difficult to see that early diagnosis of potential difficulties could be a preventive, rather than predictive, measure. The way in which such an assessment is acted upon will be the determining factor in whether or not pigeon-holing of a child occurs. Similarly, the way in which assessments are made – in familiar and varied settings, by a number of adults, all of them familiar to and with the child – will ensure that the judgements are holistic and as fair as possible. The involvement of the parents and the child in the process of the assessments is also vital, whenever possible, since their perception of what is happening will provide valuable insights into why the child performed in a particular way in a particular situation, with reflections on the ethos of any outside provision, so sensitizing professionals to their own value-laden bias.

A further fear in relation to assessment arises out of the fact that when we assess a child we must acknowledge that we are making 'best guesses'. Much of the debate about the assessment in relation to the implementation of the National Curriculum has centred around the way in which researchers who are familiar with the development of young children and with forms of assessment are the most likely people of all to express concern that there is a great deal that we do not know, that young children are individuals who will respond differently to varied situations, and that we are only just beginning to work on the effects of stereotyping. In other words, our assessments are easily affected by the hidden curriculum in which we ourselves have been educated, relating to gender, race, class and handicap. For example, a recent newspaper article about a preschool service (*Sunday Times*, 30 April 1989) quoted one member of staff as anxious that some children attending the group could not use a knife and fork. This is an example of a value-laden informal assessment. The danger is that such an assessment could be incorporated in a checklist for a group, thus giving the item an apparent seal of official approval, without any consideration of the social context or cultural make-up of the group, or reviews at a later stage when that make-up may have changed.

This naturally leads on to the question of who would keep or see such records of assessment. Debates about confidentiality and a code of conduct for all involved with young children and their families should be elements in training, irrespective of the type of institution in which the adult is to work. If such discussion has not occurred in initial training, perhaps heads of nurseries, playgroup advisers, childminders' officers, and so on, should be expected to ensure that the subject is broached. Where parents are involved in the day-to-day running of a group, the concept of confidentiality and its implications for the group should surely be a discussion point. It is only when we adults ourselves de-centre (put ourselves in the child's shoes) (Donaldson, 1978), that we begin to appreciate what it might feel like to be on the receiving end of our assessments and to appreciate that, whether we like it or not, we may be making judgements about the children with whom we are involved, judgements which, whether written down or not, are informing our actions in relation to those children or those families.

Repugnance for a system whereby a national curriculum and assessment might operate for children under five seems to stem largely from our view of childhood innocence and dilemmas about the rights and role of the family in relation to the state, allied to an assumption that the introduction of such a system would result in 'hothousing' (too early formal work). The age at which statutory schooling starts in the UK has no basis in a clear educational rationale (Woodhead, 1989), yet we are not so perturbed by the idea of making assessments of five-year-olds if it is to help match tasks to the child's ability and interests. Nor are we negative about the kinds of curricular planning and assessment which are carried out in nursery schools and classes deemed to show 'good practice' (DES, 1989). In fact, this expertise is praised. Currently there are anxieties about such matters as the pressure to teach reading in some preschool institutions; the lack of funding for training preschool workers; poor-quality provision which could develop if the needs of childminders and crèches; workers are not supported and monitored, together with the need to retain young women in the workforce. In this context we need greater awareness about a preschool curriculum based on play and exploration, first-hand experience, and with this, accompanying awareness about how we constantly assess our children. This can only be achieved by educating all involved in the field of early childhood in child development and how young children learn relating this to their own real-life interactions with the children in their work-place.

10
Staff roles, styles and development

As children pass through the education system in England and Wales or Scotland or Northern Ireland, they are likely to experience changes in the training and philosophies of those adults with whom they come into contact. Early years workers are more likely to be women (the few males who do enter this field tend to move up the career ladder rapidly), to have fewer qualifications in higher education, to receive lower pay, and to be accorded lower status than those who work with older children. If, in the case of the last two points, they are said to be simply receiving their just desserts, since all they do is play with children or mind them, it is perhaps sadly true that early years workers do not in general articulate to the world the complex and demanding, though rewarding and exciting nature of their task. In part, this lack of articulation may be due to the great variety of settings, ideology and training currently extant in the field, and it is important to examine the ways in which such factors influence practice.

Philosophy and aims of provision

It is usually assumed that all early years workers share the child-centred philosophy enshrined in the Hadow (Consultative Committee, 1933) and Plowden (CACE, 1967) reports, and that this will be reflected in their aims and practice. Webb (1974, p. 19) argued that nurseries have traditionally gained from their exclusion from the main stream of schooling and that, despite the need for constant reappraisal and evaluation to maintain effectiveness, nurseries are able to resist external pressures and to have aims essentially intrinsic to childhood rather than instrumental... most are committed to helping each child develop as a characteristic person; to offering him appropriate experiences in the present.

In studies which have solicited the views of nursery workers (for example, Taylor *et al.*, 1972; Parry and Archer, 1974; Hutt *et al.*, 1989) respondents confirm their espousal of a child-centred philosophy. This is indeed said to be reflected in their choice of aims, although there are subtle differences in emphasis. The studies reported in the early 1970s found that nursery teachers saw the social and emotional development of children as their over-arching aim. Later, Hutt *et al.* (1989) found that teachers now emphasized children's language development, while staff in social services day nurseries continued to focus their attention on the emotional development of their charges, and playgroup supervisors were more concerned about offering children opportunities to mix with others and to develop independence. Naturally enough, each group would probably hope additionally to include those aims identified as over-arching by colleagues from other sectors, and it is important to remember that any surveys of this type are attempting to tease out subtle differences. Curtis (1986) argues that forcing nursery teachers to make such a selection is unrealistic and shows misunderstanding of the nature of early childhood education, where the aims are inextricably intertwined. However, such results do highlight the ways in which current in-service courses, more prevalent in the education sector than in the others, influence the perceptions of the staff involved.

At the time of the later study there had been considerable stress placed on the development of children's language, following the work of Joan Tough (1976) and her colleagues, and this may account for the aim of language development being given a high priority at the time the research by Hutt *et al.* (1989) was carried out. One of the further aims of the teachers in the Hutt *et al.* (1989) cohort was that of helping children prepare for the infant school. Although many early years workers balk at the view that this is their primary function, as Dowling (1988) points out, the statement of aims of education, irrespective of the age of the child, should surely be that made in the Warnock Report (DES, 1978b), namely to enlarge children's knowledge, experience and understanding, and thus their awareness of moral values and capacity for enjoyment; and second, to enable them to enter the world after formal school is over as active participants in society and as responsible contributors to it. In a sense, the nursery contributes to that second aim by enabling children to move on to the infant school ready to meet each new challenge with joy and curiosity. In view of the implementation of the National Curriculum in primary and secondary schools, it is important for preschool workers to be aware of the ways in which they could influence, rather than being influenced by, such developments, for, as we saw in Chapter 9 on assessment, nursery teachers have much experience to offer colleagues in the statutory sector.

One aim given a significantly low rating by the staff in the nurseries studied by Hutt's team was that of involving parents at a partnership level in their children's education. Results from other studies (for example, Clift *et al.*, 1980; Tizard *et al.*, 1981; Ward, 1982; Wells and Burke, 1988; Pugh and De'Ath, 1989) indicate that several factors are involved. First, such involvement is, thankfully, increasing. Second, teacher trainers are now more likely to offer courses at initial and in-service level in this area. In other words, both of these points indicate an amelioration. Third, the nursery nurses in education settings are more likely to hold views more negative than those of teachers on the advantages to be gained from parental involvement in group activities – it would therefore appear that this is a managerial issue connected with feelings of vulnerability about role and status, and as such merits attention from head teachers and their teams. Finally, the effects of the National Curriculum concerning parental rights seem likely to encourage all establishments to review their aims and practices and to improve parent–teacher partnerships where necessary. It is evident from research (Ward, 1982) that parents who are given the opportunity to share in curricular decisions, observations and practical involvement are more aware of the purposes of different play activities in fostering educational progress.

The interpretation of philosophies in practice

Hutt *et al.* (1989) found that nursery teachers in their study were the most likely early years workers to emphasize their provision for children's learning needs, but that the teachers were divided as to whether this should be effected through intervention by the adults or by expecting the children to learn simply through their presence in a rich environment, with opportunities to interact with others. King (1978) postulated that certain infant teachers in his study gave more adult guidance than others as a result of the influence of the junior school ethos, as opposed to early years progressivism. King further suggested that such progressive attitudes were based on beliefs in developmentalism, individualism and childhood innocence.

What seems to be at the heart of the difficulty is the interpretation of the concept of 'child-centredness'. If a teacher believes 'child-centred' to mean providing an environment in which children pursue their own interests with no adult intervention other than that which children themselves invite, a totally free play style of setting, then it is also likely that there will be little obvious structure. (See Chapter 8 for further discussion.)

Arguing that the idea of natural child development, which underpins child-centred approaches, is, first, a social construction, second, contrary to the beliefs and experiences of working class families, and third, essentially a mode of control, since it is subject to stereotyping along class and gender lines, Walkerdine (1985) raises our awareness of value-laden judgements and bias which we should all recognize and attempt to eradicate. The very activities which are provided do impose some constraints on children's activities, and while learning itself is value-free, certain other factors – non-verbal communication, such as eye-contact, tone of voice, length of and frequency of interactions – may cause an adult's influence to be biased.

At the other extreme, in an adult-directed setting, the structure would be very obvious and rigid, with a regime geared to pushing each child through certain hoops. The intermediate position, in which a teacher is aware that there are certain societal expectations of both her and the children she teaches, but at the same time is congizant of children's individual interests and needs, child development patterns, and the ecology of the setting in which she works, there is likely to be a child-centred emphasis in which the structure is transparent. This means that such a teacher plans themes and activities, and in so doing provides resources, which, from experience, she knows the children with whom she works will find exciting and interesting. She is likely to have clear ideas about what she hopes her pupils will learn from their encounters, but she will not be bound by these alone, being prepared, open-minded, skilful, sensitive and flexible about children's potential for exploration. In this way, the teacher sees child and curriculum as interactive, not at opposite ends of a continuum.

Such a teacher maintains a transparent structure by her use of team discussions, records, displays, parental involvement, observation of children at work, evaluation, intervention and further planning. These teacher activities are not always apparent to the children or to certain visitors who may not be aware of the work which such processes involve. Bennett's (1976) study of teaching styles and pupil progress provided an example of such a teacher, and it was the children in her class who were those judged to have the highest level of achievement.

What evidence is there then of early years workers engaging children in ways which are likely to fulfil their aims?

Lubeck (1985) found that the nursery workers in the groups she studied were in fact preparing the children, through the curriculum as experienced by those respective groups of children, for life in a white middle-class neighbourhood, by encouraging individualism and competition, or for life in a black ghetto, by developing the children's identification with group needs and co-operative support.

Similarly, Speekman Klass (1986) argues that worries in the United States that daycare may lead to a weakening of American individualism are unfounded – the daycare workers she observed transmitted accepted values and fostered children's autonomy.

One cannot say whether or not these were explicitly among the aims of the workers observed, and Lubeck makes the point that, in fact, for a post-industrial society to succeed, its future citizens all need the whole range of personal and social skills being developed separately in the groups she observed. But can both individualism and a collective consciousness be developed in one person, can such skills be applied in different situations, or will one generally override the other because of the person's underpinning value system and beliefs?

In the UK it is necessary to ask not simply about the relationship between philosophy and practice but further, how children's learning is affected by the structure, teaching methods, adult–child ratio, use of space, and so on, in the different settings, and subsequently how the differing philosophy, training and status of the adults involved influences the emphasis in relating aims to practice.

Observational studies of different types of institution where under-fives are found (see, for example, Turner and Green, 1977; Garland and White, 1980; Sestini, 1987) indicate that, irrespective of allegiances (to education, social services or PPA), there are likely to be variations in the style of a group, in the sense that the structure adopted and use of space will influence the emergence of potential learning situations. They also show that the number of adults in a team is important; but it is not simply a matter of reducing the adult–child ratio and thus improving the possible frequency of adult–child interaction otherwise limited by time – indeed, the presence of too many adults can also reduce effectiveness if they begin to interact with each other more frequently than with the children. In a study of a carefully structured setting, in which staff organization and the planning of activities was prioritized by the experienced teachers and nursery nurses (Murphy, 1980; Murphy and Wilkinson, 1982), there were high levels of cognitively oriented staff-child interactions, many with the children working in groups of two to six, with an individual member of staff. Care must be taken, however, not to equate structuring and the fostering of small-group work with more direction by the adults, since the study by Sylva *et al.* (1980) indicates that a setting in which children learn through guided play is more effective than a rigid, formal regime for small children.

Further, Smith and Connolly's (1980) study indicates that, as one would expect, an increase in the number of children per adult will result in more child–child interactions; while the number of adult–child interactions will remain fairly constant, each child will be the subject of fewer interactions and there is also likely to be a qualitative reduction in those interactions. The simple fact of having a greater number of children with whom to execute managerial functions will necessarily mean that there is less time to focus on cognitively orientated interactions.

Smith and Connolly (1980) suggest that an increase in free play and child–child interactions may not always be deleterious to the children, for between the years of three and five children are becoming more peer-orientated and less adult-dependent. For children under this age the staffing ratio may be a different kettle of fish. We cannot as yet be sure what kinds of adult–child ratio are optimal. Increasing child–child interactions in free play offers opportunities to develop co-operative, group and other skills, but this must be balanced against the possibility that staff will be forced into managerial rather than educative roles.

In examining the effectiveness of adults observed at work with young children the differences in role need to be made clear and, to this end, the remainder of this chapter is devoted to evidence of the ways in which teachers and other under-fives workers differ; evidence of the effectiveness of such workers as educators of very young children, including the need to pay attention to the smooth running of a team; and the implications for early years teachers.

Teachers, nursery nurses and playgroup supervisors

Since Cass's (1975) observational study included only those teachers deemed to offer examples of 'good' nursery practice, it is necessary to turn to other studies, for example, Thomas (1973). Thomas studied talk in nursery settings; she was highly critical of the apparent inability of staff to respond sensitively to the needs of individual children, and of their repetitive use of the same activities day after day. Three years later, Tizard *et al.* (1976) painted a somewhat better picture, but there still seemed to be little really stimulating discussion between adult and child, irrespective of the avowed emphasis, educational or otherwise, of the group observed. It seems important to reiterate the point made earlier that around this time there was a belief among early years educators that, given the right environment and equipment, children needed time to explore and learn unimpeded by adult intervention. This style of working is exemplified in the work of Stallibrass (1975). It seems a strange interpretation of child-centred philosophy and would appear to be the result of a close adherence to a romantic ideology, following the ideas of Rousseau, Wordsworth and others, that society, and adults, even well-intentioned adults, would influence young children in an unhealthy, unnatural way. It may also have been the result of earlier interpretations of the theories of Jean Piaget, the Swiss zoologist turned psychologist, whose influential ideas grew out of his observations of his own children. Piaget argued that the child is an active, not a passive, learner and that children learn through interaction with their environment. Some practitioners interpreted this to mean that they should leave the child to explore and experiment, alone and uninterrupted. Curtis (1986) comments that the early pioneers, the McMillan sisters and Susan Isaacs, would have been 'horrified' had they known the way in which Piaget's work was being applied and used to justify 'cosy', undemanding schools for young children. As Nancy Elliott, Newcastle upon Tyne Senior Inspector for Primary Education commented at the 1989 Primary Education Conference in Scarborough, the lack of challenge in the curriculum offered by some early years establishments, proudly described by staff as 'happy places', makes them 'the equivalent of a lobotomy'. (Elliott, 1989).

The study by Hutt *et al*. (1989) shows that, although non-child-related activity by staff is fairly constant across the different groups, especially when outdoor play is being observed, and although teachers had slightly longer attention spans in child-centred bouts of activity, for the nursery nurses, working in a nursery school or class alongside a teacher – a setting, then, with an avowed educational intent – this was likely to produce higher levels of cognitively focused work with children, compared with similarly trained colleagues working in day nurseries. Hutt *et al*. recommended a restructuring of the nursery environment to enable staff to interact with children for more prolonged periods of time. In fact this team, along with Smith and Connolly (1980), found that children's bouts of activity were considerably longer when an adult was present than when children-only groups were involved. Furthermore Sylva *et al*. (1980) found that children experienced higher levels of cognitive challenge in activities where an adult was involved, extending the play opportunities afforded.

Due to their findings that later competence in literacy and numeracy was strongly related to preschool attainment in these areas, Tizard *et al.* (1988) attempted to tease out those aspects of nursery practice which fostered this learning. They argue (Tizard *et al.*, 1988, p. 169) 'simply introducing children to books in a happy atmosphere does not ensure that they will make a connection between meaning and print, or have any understanding of the written language'. Directing children's attention to aspects of print, writing, and so on, during activities, such as sharing a book, writing a shopping list together, disembeds that knowledge for the child and makes it accessible.

The study of staff roles and deployment by Clift *et al.* (1980) reinforces the findings of others, that interaction with individual children in the nursery is often fragmented and fleeting. Through interviews and observations, the research team collected data on staff members' perceived roles, with teachers being seen as having greater responsibility for the children's cognitive development and nursery nurses for caring aspects of the group. However, there were many similarities in behaviour relating to membership of the same team, rather than the same profession. Heaslip (1985) suggests that although the same was true for the study he carried out in Avon, it is easy to gloss over the subtle differences in role and training which can affect the adult's style of working. The earlier study had also discovered that staff would often respond to crises in a reactive way. The implications for careful planning of roles, where, depending upon the number of adults available, one will be responsible for particular activities, ensured of opportunities for prolonged interaction with individual children or small groups, while another member of staff acts as monitor, or 'troubleshooter', at the same time making careful observations of children's movements. This is vital if staff are to be able to record which children are 'cruising', that is, avoiding close contact with adults, with other children, or with certain demanding activities. With three team members, whether the third is another teacher, a nursery nurse or a parent, the potential for extended dialogue with children is greater than in settings where there has been no such planning. It also means that certain children can be targeted each week and all staff meet to discuss their observations. By rotating which member of staff plays which part in the team, different viewpoints can be acquired by every contributor to the assessment. Such developments in management, of course, also entail a restructuring of the use of equipment, to enable children to be more independent, thus freeing staff to spend more time on educative interactions. It is often surprising how quickly very young children become competent managers of equipment, space, and of any other children who are novices.

Richman and McGuire (1988) assessed the characteristics of different day nurseries and examined the links between these characteristics, the ethos of the nursery, and the behaviour of staff and children. In those institutions where senior staff were supportive, led by example, took part in nursery activities and encouraged parents to become involved, the researchers found that other staff behaved more confidently in these respects and children were less aggressive. Since day nurseries tend to have a high enrolment rate from families where staff anticipate that the children will have emotional problems, this is a complex issue. However, the study signals the importance of staff attention to the children's activities, rather than to managerial tasks (cleaning for example), and where staff are confident and encouraging to parents, there are measurable benefits to the children. In other words, the overall style of nursery organization is clearly related to staff behaviour, and this, together with staff-child ratios, affects the levels and quality of adult-child interaction.

Turner and Green's (1977) study of playgroup leaders in Belfast provides us with evidence that despite their disavowal of educational aims, playgroup personnel were devoting eight times as many interactions to cognitive as to social and emotional interactions with children. However, in the Hutt *et al.* (1989) study, the playgroup leaders had the shortest mean activity span in associative behaviour with children and the highest levels of activity not involving children (monitoring outdoor play, clearing up, and so on). The authors state that the differences in levels of associative behaviour are small, all settings being generally similar, and one might surmise that the focus of the playgroup supervisors' attention could well have been the parents themselves for a relatively high percentage of time, since playgroup sessions are short and parents are encouraged to be involved. We have no evidence that this is the case, and we must ask ourselves whether the indirect benefits to the children, through their parents, will be more valuable than through direct interaction with the supervisor. The small home playgroups reported by Osborn and Milbank (1987) to have the greatest long-term effect on preschool children seem likely to have offered those children a great deal of small group and individual interaction with a familiar adult, in a familiar (home, rather than large-building) setting. The larger playgroups did not fare so well, and these two factors – features of the buildings and adult–adult interactions taking precedence over adult–child interactions, particularly since some of the adults in a large playgroup setting may change from day to day through the parent-rota system – may well be crucial.

Those under-fives found in reception classes have been the object of much concern, and evidence from a number of studies (for example, Willes, 1983; Barrett, 1986; Stevenson, 1987; Ghayle and Pascal, 1988;

Bennett and Kell, 1989) demonstrates that here the children are subjected to a style of management which is too directive, with teachers too preoccupied with narrowly defined reading, writing and number activities. Improvements in some primary schools, where head teachers and staff have been willing to learn from nursery colleagues, have gained the approval of HMI (DES, 1989).

Perhaps the use of the metaphor of one style (observed in the infant school) being 'too big' and another (in nurseries) being 'too small' is apt. The style which would be 'just right' would be between the two – not rigid, but not *laissez-faire*, not adult-directed but not without high expectations.

Effective adult–child interactions

Further examination of the research evidence (for example, Wood *et al.*, 1980; Tizard and Hughes, 1984; Meadows and Cashdan, 1988; Hutt *et al.*, 1989) concerning the types of interaction workers have with young children seems to indicate that, far from such dialogue being intellectually stimulating, it is often banal and cursory, requiring children to answer closed questions, provide labels and, as one child has put it, 'tell the teacher something they already know'.

What these studies seem to suggest is that workers should behave more like parents do when they interact with their offspring sharing an activity. Tizard and Hughes (1984) go so far as to add that, contrary to the belief widely held during the years of 'compensatory education', working-class parents are well able to sustain dialogue with their children and to extend their children's experience in the process. What is sadly also likely, however, is the fact that working-class parents are unaware of their role in so educating their children, and, furthermore, when they do set out to 'teach' their child something they perceive as educational (such as reading), they will expect only to achieve this through 'educational' texts (Davie *et al.*, 1984).

Using the ideas of the post-Piagetians, Vygotsky's (1978) 'zone of proximal development' and Wood *et al.*'s (1976) metaphor of 'scaffolding', Wood (1986) and Meadows and Cashdan (1988) follow the line of potential staff development set by Wood *et al.* (1980), that adults working with young children must be aware of four factors in their own and the child's behavioural repertoire in order to maximize learning in any situation.

First, teachers should work diagnostically, observing, listening to and assessing each child's level of competence before diving in and asking questions, since the questioning may otherwise be at too low or too high a level – a session spent with a child who could correctly answer every question posed, without effort, may be as much of a waste of time for both parties as one where a child could answer none. Although a sensitive teacher will try to enable a child to be successful, enhancement of the child's self-esteem and learning will only occur if challenging questions are tackled, and with the adult's help this is probable. Further, discussing some shared experience, rather than having a prolonged discussion about a topic of which the teacher has little knowledge, actually helps the adult scaffold the experience for the child.

For example, a teacher might relate to the child her own childhood memory of a visit to Blackpool illuminations, offering the child opportunities to ask questions, rather than asking closed questions about the child's trip, or trying to eke out a conversation about some incident during this family's outing, of which the teacher has no evidence.

Second, it is important for teachers to plan resources so that activities are meaningful and worthwhile to small children, encouraging them to take part in the running of the group. For example, making a snack of raw fruit and vegetables for others to share, discussing classification of fruit and vegetables in this way, will be much more relevant to the child than some sorting of mathematical symbols, and will engender a wider range of dialogue.

Third, part of the provision of the scaffolding will be assisting children in developing an awareness of their own skills and knowledge, what they can do and what they know, and how to go about gaining more knowledge and skills. It may be as simple as saying aloud to themselves the sequence of a task. This sort of 'knowing' is what psychologists call 'metacognition'. Nelson (1986) has also developed the idea of 'scripts'. These help the child in much the same way as an adult's 'scaffolding' of a task makes it more manageable to the child, since the 'script' provides the known structure to a set of events, much like a good story, so that details can be slotted in and attended to, the basic 'script' being already familiar to the child.

Fourth, adopting an apprenticeship approach with young children means that the adult can share in the child's intentions, allowing for the child to take control of and, in the current jargon, 'to own' his or her learning. What the adult can provide is the structure to the situation by helping the child decide on an appropriate goal, directing or focusing attention on the meaningful parts of the activity. For example, if preparing the snack mentioned earlier, she might help the child decide how to ensure there is a fair share of each fruit or vegetable on each group's plate, how to check that each plate contains some of each item, and so on. Providing children with opportunities to recall such actions is, furthermore, moving them along the way towards what Donaldson (1978) called 'disembedded' thinking, freedom to apply abstract concepts to other situations and contexts different from those in which they were originally developed.

This style of working means a rejection of both romantic and cultural transmission models of education. The Romantics believe that children will learn through contact with a rich environment, their emotional development being of paramount importance. The cultural transmission model portrays children as empty vessels waiting to be topped up, so a didactic style of teaching would be adopted by its adherents. The 'reflective practitioner' (Pollard and Tann, 1987), a teacher whose approach is based on the work of Dewey (1933), has a commitment to integrating the emotional with the cognitive, social and moral education of children. She sees her role as fostering construction on the part of the child, as opposed to instruction by herself, and developing autonomy and co-operation, rather than using coercion and demanding obedience.

Probably the most difficult aspect of this for an adult to learn is the relinquishing of control. Helping children become independent learners takes time, especially if those children are accustomed to adult regulation, and even more so where members of a staff team have not had time to discuss the role, responsibility, and resource implications of such strategies.

Additionally, the issue of unsupported reception class teachers, reported sympathetically by Desforges and Cockburn (1987, p. 137) to be adopting as classroom routines survival strategies 'which could hardly be less well designed for the development of higher order thinking', leads one to plead for more classroom aides, while at the same time advocating that they try the techniques reported in Meadows and Cashdan (1988). This study describes the way in which a teacher takes the starting point of a literary theme, a story (in the example *Watership Down*), and allows the children to choose activities in which they explore aspects of the theme. Certainly it would be worthwhile evaluating the adoption of such strategies in different settings. Research on the development of children's thinking in the early years of schooling appears unequivocal.

Evidence for the vital impact an adult can have in the cognitively focused play situation comes from the work of Bruner (1986), Smith (1986). An adult nearby can provide starting points, support, response and follow-up reviews, along with cognition developed through social interaction, even in situations where the adult intervention, owing to high numbers of children, is through the transparent structures of resource provision and organization. The majority of interactions at the time of the activity may be child–child (see Doise and Mugny, 1984).

Effective teamwork

The moulding of a group of assorted adults, be they all from the same professional background or not, is often difficult and painful. For, as Corbishley (1984) has remarked, adults are sometimes irrational and they have emotions which are inclined to get in the way of logical behaviour. The study already cited, by Clift *et al*. (1980) and that by Ferri *et al*. (1981) provide overwhelming evidence of the differences in perceptions and role expectations of teachers and nursery nurses. The HMI report on combined nursery centres (DES, 1988a) stressed the need for management lines to be clear and for conditions of work and salaries to be fair. They state that when similar conditions apply to the differently trained staff, good relations are more likely.

Heaslip (1988) has provided a list of the experienced and perceived grievances of nursery nurses; these include salary, status and career prospects. Nursery nurses working alongside teachers are the group most likely to express resentment of parental involvement in group activities (Ward, 1982). It seems likely that this is so in settings where such involvement means an erosion of their own role and thus status. Teachers need to be aware of this effect and to help nursery assistants and other classroom aides be involved in inducting the parents into the purpose of the nursery activities. Further, Heaslip (1987) has expounded the view that nursery teachers are often untrained and unprepared for leading a team. The nursery teacher should, he suggests, be made aware of the grievances of the nursery nurses as well as having developed skills to enable the professional development of their teams.

At a time when there are calls for greater co-ordination of services for under-fives and their families, it is imperative that nursery teachers are provided with in-service courses which foster their learning with and about the other professionals – social workers, doctors, health visitors, and those working in the voluntary sector, such as playgroup leaders and childminders – with whom they need to co-operate. Watt's (1977) research exemplified the levels of difficulty experienced by the parents of young children trying to make sense of the mess that is preschool provision. Teachers in that study were unfortunately guilty of retreating behind a façade of professionalism and so keeping both families and colleagues from other services at arm's length. It is only through courses at which teachers develop their own professionalism, their ability to articulate what they do and why, that they will also develop supportive networks, all of which will give them the confidence to work openly with others – the nursery nurses with whom they share their daily tasks, the parent with whom they share the children, the governors with whom they share the school, and the other professionals with whom they share a concern for society and the experiences of its future citizens. While few parents wish to be involved in management (Ward, 1982; Pugh and De'Ath, 1989) the majority wish to be valued, listened to and taken seriously. Even in centres where partnership is encouraged, Pugh and De'Ath (1989, p. 59) found that

> it appeared difficult to move away from an imbalance of power . . . it is only too easy for staff to present an issue as an area in which parents can make decisions, and yet the professional is only prepared to accept one option.

As well as being aware of the need for personal and professional development of the staff team, the nursery teacher should be sensitive to the conditions which can lead to staff 'burnout'. It is easy to trivialize the work of a nursery teacher because of the usually curious and exploring nature of young children: the way in which highly motivated young children will engage in play and exploration makes the work look simple, especially in a group where the adult expertise is almost unobservable, seeming so natural and unobtrusive. Whitebrook *et al.* (1982), whose evidence admittedly derives from US nursery centres, contend that there are many factors which can lead to very stressful conditions for early years staff, among them the personalities of the staff (they are likely to be self-critical idealists); the nature of the work (demands may vary from day to day); the conditions in the setting (for example, adult–child ratios, lack of breaks and free time to plan as a team); job security and changes (this might also be experienced by childminders); status; career expectations and pay. The latter point is particularly relevant in the UK, where the career and pay prospects of nursery nurses are poor compared to those of teachers, while nursery teachers themselves are subjected to relatively low levels of pay, status and promotion prospects within the teaching profession, a profession which is itself said to be at a low ebb at present.

Implications for adults working with under-fives

Current shortages of early years teachers, the planned increase in mothers of young children in the workforce and lack of government commitment to the provision of educare facilities mean that all those involved with young children, whether as providers of services or as parents, must pool expertise. The development of facilities, such as childminding, crèches, private nurseries, could be attached in satellite fashion to a nursery school or centre, so that the teachers assist in the educational aspects of provision, both at the centre and as trainers of co-workers. The valuable role of this highly trained professional can then be maximized, but it will only be so if teachers adopt democratic team approaches with colleagues, with due respect for their roles. The difficulties encountered when teachers work with those from other professions, or with voluntary workers and parents have been well documented (see Cleave *et al.*, 1982; Watt, 1977).

To work in this way will require the early years teacher to develop her effectiveness as a team leader, realizing that simply putting workers from different backgrounds together will not succeed on good will alone. There should be opportunities for all workers to come together and honestly put forward their views about their own status, conditions and feelings, as well as considerations of the management of the group, individual children's progress and other related issues.

Atkin and Webb (1985) list, as aspects of nursery management essential to the leader of a team, the ability to plan, liaise, allocate, motivate, train, monitor and innovate. A teacher with these skills, added to those she needs as an educator – understanding child development, interpreting the curriculum into meaningful activities for young children, having the ability to match her interactions with children to their individual needs, at the same time articulating to parents what she does and why and encouraging them to recognize their essential part in their child's education – fulfils a demanding professional role.

Margaret McMillan (1930), the great nursery pioneer, wanted nursery teachers to teach children by interacting with them, so extending their thinking and language. She believed that nurseries should be home-like places, happy, informal, yet stimulating. She wrote, in 1914, that nursery teachers should be remarkable for their power and their gentleness. Paterson (1911) another early writer on the role quoted by Steedman (1988), detailing his observations of London infant teachers, believed women to be ideal for such work, due to their 'mothering instinct'. Steedman (1988) has argued that Froebel's dictum that a teacher of young children should be the 'mother made concious' presents a difficulty for those who teach working-class children, for this mother made conscious is a middle-class ideal of motherhood. Indeed, I would add that she is not only expected to be mother to the child, but mother to the mothers in the case of her contacts with working-class families. Such a role was further perpetuated during the mid-twentieth century, when the inadequate family was seen as the root of all under-achievement, and compensatory education programmes were put into action. More recent research for example (Davie *et al.*, 1984; Tizard and Hughes, 1984; Wells, 1985) has shown that working-class parents, on their home ground, are by no means 'inadequate', yet in the group setting children from working-class families are likely to lose out. The implication would appear to be that this middle-class 'mother made conscious' is the root of the failure, for perhaps she is overbearing, unfamiliar and unapproachable. How might the teacher remedy such a situation? First, does she know the child and parents well, making them feel 'at home' and comfortable in the group and in her presence? It is often the extra-curricular activities with parents which foster a more equal partnership, a feeling of friendship and trust. Second, what do the parents and the teacher do for or with the child and how will they help the child achieve his or her goals? If one brainstorms the list of what a parent does for a child and alongside it the same exercise with teachers as the focus, it is surprising how similar the lists turn out to be. It is true that in the areas of continuous assessment, recording, and systematic planning for fostering the child's future learning needs, the teacher's role differs from that of parent. It is also true that in other areas, such as providing food and shelter, the intensity of the parents' responsibility is of a higher order than that of the teacher. But in essence the roles are very similar. That is not to say that the teacher should try in any way to usurp the parent – quite the reverse!

The important point here is that the teacher of young children should not rest on her laurels, believing that being like a good parent is enough; she must develop her professional expertise in the ways discussed earlier, evaluating her effectiveness in her interactions with children, by using tape recordings, video recordings, and the observations of trusted colleagues. 'Early years practitioners must dispel the myth that the precise virtue of the mother-made-conscious is that she doesn't have to be very clever' (Steedman, 1988, p. 92).

Belotti (1975) analyses the predominance of female staff in the Italian nursery field, suggesting that here we find the approved feminine virtues of timidity, conservatism, triviality and anti-intellectualism. In a society where 'normality' is measured against the standard of the adult male – assertive, intelligent, articulate – it is a small step to rationalize women workers and the young children in their groups out of any consideration for priority treatment.

Steedman (1988) speculates on the possible effects which such attitudes to the type of women seen as a suitable early years worker may be having on children during their most formative years. Walkerdine's (1985) observations of a particular nursery teacher led her to conclude that the effect is a negative one as far as developing a less sexist society is concerned.

There have been cases recently where governing bodies have sought to appoint to a nursery teaching post a candidate whom they saw as 'motherly'. At the other end of the primary school spectrum, infant/first school women heads lost out in selections to male middle school heads when reorganization to primary schools occurred. It would appear that in the community women teachers are expected to be maternal, gentle and caring, and male teachers hard disciplinarians. The person-orientation favoured by most women workers is a strength, but it should not be allowed to impede the practice of a team. If, for example, one member of the team puts forward at a planning meeting an idea which is inappropriate at that time, it should be possible for the team to acknowledge the idea, suggesting it be saved for later, without any feelings of rejection on the part of the worker involved – it is not the person herself but the set of conditions her idea would produce for the children which is being shelved.

If early childhood workers accept the stereotyped view of themselves they are unlikely to be 'hard' in the sense of expecting high standards of children, confronting controversial issues and maintaining a determination to achieve their aims. Being 'hard' in such a way does not mean becoming a less caring human being.

If we wish to see work with under-fives taken seriously as education, but with care inextricably linked, we must encourage more men to enter and to remain in the field, and the women attracted to this work must become conscious of and articulate about the educational, as well as the caring, aspects of the role.

11
Involving parents

Although earlier studies (such as Douglas, 1964) had already documented the influence of parental attitudes to education upon the achievements of their children, it was not until after the publication of the Plowden Report (CACE, 1967) that 'parental involvement' became an issue for schools. The Plowden Committee had commissioned a survey of parents of primary school children, from which it was concluded that parents' attitudes had a greater influence on educational achievements than any of the other factors considered. Later research (Rutter *et al.*, 1979) showed that the school did in fact play a considerable part in enhancing (or preventing) children's chances of reaching their potential. Meanwhile the Taylor (DES, 1977) and Warnock (DES, 1978b) reports and subsequent legislation in 1980, 1981 and recently in the 1988 Education Act, contributed to the widening recognition that parents should have greater involvement in their children's education and in the management of the schools they attended.

Early pioneers, most notably Margaret McMillan, had stressed the importance of the parental role and the relationships between parents and the school. Shortly after the Second World War when 'No parents beyond this gate' signs were common, teachers expressed their support for the notion of parental involvement in their children's education (Wall, 1947), and one wonders what their interpretation of the phrase could have been. Similarly, today, there are no doubt many differing views of what is and what might, or should, be in the name of parental involvement.

A further impetus to the growth of parental involvement came from the formation of the playgroup movement in 1961. As the PPA grew, in both numbers and strength, so a cohort of parents, largely mothers, expressed their dissatisfaction with the feeling that they were excluded from their children's educational experiences once they moved on to a maintained school. Those teachers who realized the potential of partnerships, many of them women who had been involved in the playgroup scene themselves, were eager to take up what parents offered. The only problem was that the playgroup movement drew most of its support from middle-class families and, with the EPA provision and extra resourcing for nurseries being focused on working-class areas, many parents were not given the opportunity to engage in an equivalent experience to boost their confidence during the preschool years.

There were exceptions in some working-class areas, such as the Red House EPA project (Smith, 1975). Even in middle-class areas, some playgroups did not offer parents the variety of experiences and support that may be necessary to set up the autonomous child–parent dyad advocated by Bronfenbrenner (1977). In Bronfenbrenner's (1977) system the preschool worker becomes a facilitator, fostering the parents' abilities as primary educators.

The idea that a triangle of child, parent and teacher builds the strongest structure for the child's education is widely accepted, but the question we need to ask is what kind of triangle. Does the child actually make decisions? Are parents given the opportunity to become involved in all aspects of the child's education? What do teachers and other preschool workers interpret as parental involvement?

Torkington (1986) has suggested that there are three types of parental involvement: school-focused, curriculum-focused, and parent-focused. By *school-focused* she means approaches where the parents help the school achieve goals such as developing a fund-raising Parent-Teacher Association, help with sports arrangements, fêtes, and so on. Her *curriculum-focused* approaches would include parental involvement in the development of children's cognitive skills, such as learning to read, or, for preschoolers, teacher-initiated preparation for school such as sorting and classifying objects at home. The third type of involvement, *parent-focused* seen by Torkington as the nearest to partnership, like Brofenbrenner's autonomous dyad, gives the parents support in knowing and understanding their own children's development and learning, together with assistance in developing their own skills, confidence, knowledge and abilities. This type of approach starts with the assumption that not only are parents the people who know their own children best, but also they are in a position to complement the teacher's role. This last point is extremely important, since many of those who are against certain forms of parental involvement suggest that parents would usurp the teachers and that parents in classrooms would put the jobs of the professionals at risk (see, for example, Cyster *et al.*, 1980).

Three categories similar to those of Torkington are proposed by Cunningham and Davis (1985): the *expert* model, in which the parents have a peripheral role and control remains in the hands of the staff; the *transplant* model, in which it is recognized that parents do have some talents which are of worth and can be enlisted to the advantage of the children; and the *consumer* model, in which the parents ultimately make the decisions. Cunningham and Davis (1985) point out that if partnership is the goal, then the expectations of parents and staff need to be made explicit. The history of parental involvement in the education sector has generally been one of haziness and haphazard arrangements, with positive effects often arising out of serendipity rather than good planning and an overt understanding of human behaviour. Some local authorities and schools are now accepting the need for discussion of parental involvement policy, with negotiated roles being laid down as part of a policy statement.

A number of research studies have indicated that both the practice of and attitudes towards parental involvement are variable. In general, parents are more likely to feel they have a role in preschool institutions than in the schools catering for older pupils. There are also many factors which appear to influence the strategies adopted; for example, working-class parents are less likely to be involved in the school's activities than their middle-class counterparts. Schools with low staffing, open-plan buildings, and integrated curricula were more in favour of parents working alongside teachers, whereas pupils' ethnic origins and maternal employment did not influence the levels of involvement either way (Cyster *et al.*, 1980).

During the ten years which followed the publication of the Plowden Report, many preschool studies were carried out, some of them action research programmes, including a few which were unashamedly compensatory, like the Head Start programmes in the USA. Smith (1980) describes short- and long-term projects, in the UK and the USA, and her survey of the organization and experience of involvement showed that two-thirds of the parents who had not been involved in their children's groups would have enjoyed the opportunity to contribute. Smith found a mismatch between parental expectations of different forms of provision and staff objectives and practice. It had not been the intention of her project to determine the possibility of long-term gains from any of the forms of involvement, or even whether such gains in educational achievement could be realized through parental involvement. Evidence for any long-term impact of parental involvement comes from

126 Educare for the under-fives

Berruetta-Clement *et al*. (1984) in the USA and from Osborn and Milbank (1987) in Great Britain. The latter study suggests that there is a strong correlation between preschool experience and later test performance on a broad range of cognitive and educational skills, and, independently of the type of preschool group attended, the participation of parents in group activities contributed to children's higher scores on the tests. Sadly, there was a discrepancy between types of group in the levels of parent participation, with approximately half of the children in hall playgroups having their parents participate, compared with just over one in eight of LEA nursery parents.

The forms parental involvement in a preschool group might take vary from those which Plowden recommended as contributing to 'better communication', such as non-educational mending, helping with craft and library corners (CACE, 1967; DES, 1975) to discussion of the curriculum, and – in the light of the 1988 Education Act – as part of the National Curriculum proposals, monitoring that curriculum and the effectiveness of the teaching.

Various studies (see, for example, Smith, 1980; Ferri *et al*., 1981; Tizard *et al*., 1981; Blatchford *et al*., 1982; Davie *et al*., 1984) have shown that parents are very keen to support their children's educational needs, but that they often lack the confidence or knowledge to do so, or to ask the most pertinent questions in order to gain such information.

A study by Ward (1982), focusing on the views of parents and staff of children in playgroups and nursery schools, found that parents expressed overwhelmingly their desire to be informed by the staff of how their child was progressing (in detail) and further, to be involved in day-to-day group activities. Only one parent in twenty wished to take on a managerial role, either as a school governer or playgroup committee member. Lilian Katz quoted in Pugh and De'Ath (1989) would no doubt see such results as perfectly logical, in the light of her summary of how parents and professionals relate to children, with parents displaying a high degree of emotional attachment, partiality and thus irrationality, whereas professionals can afford to be detached and must be seen to be impartial.

Tizard *et al*. (1981) found that the presence of parents in the playroom during sessions was no guarantee that they would become informed of the learning which was expected to take place during free play, despite staff efforts to communicate their intentions. Ward (1982) questioned staff and parents in nursery school and playgroup settings about different activities. As one might expect, the teachers were most *au fait* with the educational rationale for certain play activities, followed closely by the nursery nurses who worked alongside them. The playgroup supervisors and playgroup parents gave closely matched reasons for, say, the presence of sand or painting or fantasy play provision, but the nursery parents, most of them excluded from whole-session involvement, seemed to believe that most of these activities were provided just for fun and that the activities they saw as having the greatest importance were books, communal lunch/dinner times, and whole-group music sessions – activities they interpreted as preparation for 'big school'.

Some playgroup workers and head teachers find it strange that after twenty years the case for parental involvement is still being argued. Perhaps there are a number of reasons why parental involvement is interpreted in so many ways and in some establishments parents are kept at arm's length by an invisible sign, rather than a board declaring 'No parents beyond this point' or 'Please ring to make an appointment to see the Head'. The first reason for staff reluctance is fear due to lack of training. Some preschool workers feel inadequate to cope with the demands they imagine will be made of them. Generally, they stress that they consider their role to be that of child educator, not parent supporter. Therefore, one of the first needs is for in-service and initial training to develop all the skills needed, such as managerial skills (so that the group can be organized in a way which affords parents a real participatory role, staff can allocate time to talk to them, and other staff do not feel their role is being eroded). Other training to build staff confidence would be in communication skills, since there is no point in inviting parents to participate and then making them feel they are neither being listened to nor made welcome. While staff training in counselling skills would also be beneficial, it might be worth thinking of running counselling development sessions in which parents could take part – after all, parents are often cast in the role of counsellor to other parents, and sometimes to staff. Unfortunately, professionals have been led to believe that they should not display their own problems at work, and most of the time this is a good rule – but it can sometimes lead to much closer relationships if parents are allowed to see that staff are human!

Staff may resist parent–teacher sharing because they feel they are the trained professionals and if parents can do the job of educating their children just as well as – or even better than – they can, then what was all that training for? Here we can look back to Torkington's argument in favour of complementary roles for parent and teacher – the teacher or other trained worker does indeed have the expertise and training, the professional knowledge; the parent, on the other hand, has the most intimate knowledge of the child. By working in concert, they can offer the child the most comprehensive educational experience. After all, if one composes a list of the provisions one might hope a parent could offer a child and compare that with an equivalent list for a teacher, as suggested earlier, apart from aspects of diagnostic assessment and record-keeping, and to some extent the method of offering the experiences, the two lists would be fairly comparable. Pringle (1974) suggested that children have four basic needs: love and security; new experiences; praise and recognition; and responsibility. Pringle adds that the relative importance of these factors and the ways in which they should be met changes with the different stages of growth of the children. However, these needs do not alter according to whether the child is at home or at school.

Probably the most difficult challenge for staff in meeting the demands of parental involvement is within themselves – in their reluctance to give up their position of power. Evaluating our own practices and deciding that it is in us that change needs to occur is very painful. It can also be a slow process. We need time to discuss our thoughts with sympathetic others, time to develop strategies within a supportive network. Most people who work in preschool groups – and in schools, too – who are against the practice of parental involvement are often those with very little confidence in themselves, fearing their imagined faults will at last be found out, but outwardly blustering a host of other excuses for not trying. A further aspect of the power issue is that of the different status of staff members. Those who are paid less and given less recognition for their efforts will be the most likely to oppose parent participation in the group, since they have most to lose – which is not much to start with, but it is all they have! This means that staff will need to examine roles and relationships within the staff team, too. It is not surprising, however, that many staff teams have held negative attitudes towards the development of parental involvement, since few schemes have been publicly supported and few local authorities have appointed advisers to encourage such work. Mortimore and Mortimore (1985) stress the view that staff may believe that their workload will be increased, rather than recognizing potential benefits. Pugh and De'Ath (1989) discuss the difficulties which arise from the very nature of the role of 'people workers', such as teachers, social workers and others, whose role is different from that of a traditional 'professional' in that 'people workers' are expected to act as catalysts, developing skills and encouraging change in others. This analysis supports the argument in Chapter 10, where the idea of 'the mother made conscious' was discussed. 'People workers' are expected to care, but they are increasingly expected to empower others rather than taking over their roles. Defining where one role ends (the teacher's) and the other begins (the parent's) may be a dilemma at times. Teachers working in home-based support for children with special educational needs are particularly prone to doubts about the fairness of overloading parents with responsibilities. Is this true parental partnership, or a way of cutting down the costs of teams of supportive professionals?

Schemes in which parental empowerment has been a central aim (see Cochran, 1986; Pugh *et al.*, 1987), could often fail if parents were seen as deficient and inadequate. Staff needed to start from a position of regarding families as having some strengths, that a variety of family structures were operational and viable, that the community as a whole had a great deal of knowledge about childrearing and children, and that cultural differences were equally valued. Empowerment then becomes a dynamic process. This means that staff relationships will be forced to change. An offshoot of such a process will also be the effect upon relationships between staff in the preschool group and other professionals, since all these workers are potentially supporting the family in the empowerment process rather than usurping the roles of parents.

Once parents find their voice, they may well begin to express disappointment, as well as delight, with the service they and their children receive. In a survey conducted by Ward (1982), the contrast between the views of the playgroup parents, who knew the practices in their children's groups, and the nursery parents, who did not see much of what went on, was stark – the latter could not name a single feature of the nurseries of which they disapproved, whereas the playgroup parents named several. It would be somewhat naive to assume that this difference could be attributed to the nursery parents' utter satisfaction with everything.

Lack of knowledge could also explain many of the differences in levels of satisfaction found between ethnic groups in the ILEA (1985a) study, a view supported by Joly (1986), who sought the opinions of Mirpuri parents in Birmingham. Tomlinson (1980) suggests that the parents she questioned during the mid-1970s did not understand the British education system because most of them had themselves been educated in colonial India, East Africa or the West Indies (where, for instance, only primary education was available for most children, because it was assumed that the pupils would then go to work on the plantations). However, all the studies show that minority group parents are keen that their children should do well and would appreciate more opportunities to understand the school's methods. Many of the Asian and Afro-Caribbean parents of the early 1990s will themselves have been through the British education system. Sadly, an unfairly large proportion will have memories of poor treatment at the hands of white teachers (Eggleston *et al.*, 1986), since the research evidence shows that black pupils have often been wrongly placed in low-achievement and non-examination groups during their secondary schooling.

The need for dialogue between parents and staff is vital, since there is likely to be a mismatch between parental and staff views about the aims and methods of education, no matter where the group is. Parental involvement may take many forms, depending upon the needs and wishes of the community served, and some of that involvement may be seen as parental education in the sense of empowerment. The problem with such an outcome is that a great deal of the responsibility for the children's education is then passed back to parents, and with it the possibility of blame if the children do not reach expected levels of achievement. It would be ironic if such blame occurred when the intention was to share supportively.

Since in most cases it is mothers who work with, in and for preschool groups, this blame would be laid at their feet. Unfortunately, while most projects show some gains in children's achievements as a result of parental (which is to say, mainly maternal) involvement, such schemes also reaffirm the idea that women should be at home with their young children, and not out working (David, 1980). The four general principles suggested by Eisenstadt (1985), intended to improve services for young children and their families, rather than 'improving' the parents, would demand the dynamic relationships mentioned earlier. They are: that both parents and staff know and understand the ways in which families can control their use of the group, and which issues are negotiable; that staff work honestly and willingly to share and carry out decisions, even those they may have opposed; that parents involved in managing the service understand both the aims of the group and their ability to suggest changes in those aims if they so wish; and that, although all users may be involved, differences in circumstances will be respected, and it is acknowledged that individual involvement may vary during the time of family attachment to the service.

Following his review of parental participation in education in the European Community, Macbeth (1984) suggested that a 'school and family concordat' be instituted, in which parents signed a 'contract' in return for a school place. This contract would delineate ways in which parents' co-operation with the school would be relied upon, and in return, schools would have an obligation to liaise with parents and to ensure that mutual commitments were understood and underpinned a friendly collaborative exercise.

Conclusion

Can we conclude that the child – parent – teacher triangle exists? If it does exist, can it be demonstrated to benefit the children?

Pugh *et al.* (1987) report on many varied schemes throughout the UK in which people are working hard to achieve a balanced triangle, one in which the worker and the parent share in the child's education. There are examples of successful parental involvement in school-focused work (NCPTA reports); examples of successful curriculum-focused work (for example, at primary school level, Tizard *et al.*, 1981; Hannon and Cuckle, 1984; MacLeod, 1985); and examples of successful parent-focused projects (for example, Radin, 1972; Lazar and Darlington, 1982). What cannot be claimed is the existence of universal, flexible and varied parental involvement. Pugh and De'Ath (1989) suggest that there has been considerable development during the 1980s. However, in order to comment upon the efficacy of such involvement where it does exist, Pugh and De'Ath (1989) attempted to tease out some of the factors which fostered the development of working relationships which were ultimately of benefit to the children on whose behalf they were initiated. As a result of their research, they suggest that there are ten key elements which can either help or hinder partnership. These are: the type, function and overall philosophy of the preschool group (whether the aim is support or intervention); the establishment of a parental partnership policy; management (with parents enabled in participation at managerial levels); funding (parental partnership requires the commitment of some funding, for staff, resources, and so on); premises (location, accessibility, welcome, facilities for parents); time (to train staff, to listen to parents, to visit other centres, to enable work to develop at an appropriate pace, to persuade other colleagues about disputed aspects of the work, to evaluate and plan); the methods and strategies adopted to foster the relationship (skills in face-to-face and written contacts, involvement in play activities and curriculum discussions, attention to the needs of working parents); staff development and attitude change; training, support and supervision made available; and parental attitudes and interest.

In this chapter I have not discussed the role of home-visiting, nor offered suggestions for new ways of communicating, such as videos of the children during group sessions which working parents might borrow. The first steps towards the partnership must be made by staff, perhaps beginning by offering a warm friendship and attempting to demystify the curriculum by encouraging parents to try different activities with their children. What happens after that will depend upon those involved. It could be something apparently purely for adults, an exercise club perhaps. One head teacher who worked with such a group found that the boost to parental morale and the friendships which developed – between parent and parent, and parent and staff member – achieved far more for the education of the children in their nursery than years of open evenings and parents' workshops could have done without this as the starting point, for the conversation flowed naturally and it was when the parents felt confident that they began to discuss their views of the education which was taking place during the nursery sessions.

We have entered an era when schools are being asked to 'deliver' the curriculum. The education of children is not comparable with the provision of factory-produced materials. The future implementation of the National Curriculum will require much of parents. It is important that good home–school partnerships are formed as early as possible and that the complexity of any relationships involving emotional commitment is recognized. It is during the preschool years that the foundations can be laid.

12
Learning from other countries

The lives of young children throughout the world, and particularly those in countries which, like the United Kingdom are 'post-industrial' societies, is a theme of constant interest to early years educationists. Although a multitude of variables would make any direct transfer of systems or policies impracticable, comparisons of similarities and differences, whether of policy or practice, help us to reflect more deeply on provision in the UK.

In the report *Caring for Children*, CERI (1982, p. 4) it is claimed that:

> A new awareness of children, whether it be on the part of society in general or within the family is developing ... Nowadays, sending children to school at the age of six no longer seems enough, and there is general acceptance that learning begins long before this age. This belief, combined with other factors favouring preschool (mothers in the workforce, desire for peer relationships), have resulted in an increased nursery attendance ... today more and more levels of the population are becoming aware of the importance of the education of young children and want appropriate forms of preschool facilities to be provided for their own.

The effects of the economy on preschool provision

The collection of data and information about preschool provision world-wide is a slow and time-consuming process, although one would hope that organizations such as OMEP may ultimately, with the help of technological advances and given sufficient funding, be able to update changes and computerize details of the systems operating in different countries. Much of the information currently available was collected during the mid-1970s. The children represented by these statistics will now be nearing the end of their school careers. Furthermore, this intervening period has witnessed a recession, the effects of which have been felt by most of the industrialized economies, particularly those lacking their own fossil-fuel resources. The recession is blamed for subsequent rises in inflation, unemployment and falls in the gross national product. It has been suggested that the 'knock-on' effects of these events have been attacks on education systems and changes in the defence strategies offered by educationists in the face of competition for resources; possible competition for resources between state-funded and private provision; emphasis on levels of post-compulsory schooling and higher education; and discussion of length of schooling in the light of restricted budgets (Wirt and Harmann, 1986).

We are no longer surprised by the notion that the international community is interdependent. The relationships between young children and their parents and between the family and the state in one nation have consequences for all. Those governments which have retained their will to provide education and care facilities for the youngest children despite the effects of the recession, are those with a firm belief in the importance of the early years in relation to the individual's contribution to the state in the future, and those which either need the women workers currently engaged in the workforce or believe in the democratic rights they have already set up, ensuring that women are not expected to take on single-handedly the burden of childcare. Unfortunately, an accurate interpretation of the entries and data in the *International Yearbook of Education* (1980) is complicated by omissions and differences in terminology relating to preschool education, but several startling features emerge. The first feature is the high levels of preschool provision in the Arab states and the Eastern bloc, in comparison with Western Europe, USA, Canada and Oceania. The second is differences within Europe itself. The UK still retains its position as one of the most inadequate providers of early childhood facilities in 1988. We know all too well that the reason for inaction following the DES (1972) White Paper was the looming recession. The third feature is the entries relating to teacher training, with, for example, some countries claiming that their preschool and primary (but not secondary) trainee teachers cover courses in the country's ideology, others that their trainee early years teachers are mainly young women who study subjects like home economics but no science, and still others not even mentioning teacher training.

Like the UK, there are countries which claim that their lack of policy for nursery provision is due to a belief that it is not the job of the government to assist women to go out to work, when their proper place, according to the prevailing ideology, is in the home. The fact that there is an Equal Opportunities Act in force and an Equal Opportunities Commission, in existence in the UK since 1975 seems to have been overlooked in relation to parenting. Another argument which has been put forward is the notion that vulnerable young children would be put at the mercy of teachers who would indoctrinate them were they to spend long hours in a preschool establishment. This argument is, after all, the other side of the coin of the current policy of offering daycare places to children of families considered to be 'inadequate'; it is also a reiteration of the Jesuit claim 'Give me a child until he is seven and I will give you the man' (*sic*), a belief which appears to be outwardly adhered to in many of the communist countries of the world, since these were the nations which drew attention to the ideological content of training courses for early years practitioners. One wonders how such teacher training programmes have been affected by recent events in Eastern Europe.

During the Cultural Revolution in China, reports reaching the West made us aware of the way in which the youngest nursery school children were taught dances and dramatic enactments of political rhetoric, which shocked us in their blatancy. On our television screens we were shown four-year-olds enacting the beating of 'Uncle Sam and his running dogs'. Perhaps we were too blind or too stubborn to see that in our own system political messages were being transmitted through the hidden curriculum which were equally insidious.

Liang (Liang and Shapiro, 1983) was a small child during the 1960s. His story, beginning with his time in a Changsha nursery centre like those of many others who have been small children during times of political fervour, reassures us that the indoctrination argument against the provision of nursery education is false.

> Once when I was nearly four, I decided to escape from the child-care center . . . The child-care center was hateful . . . The songs and dances – like 'Sweeping the floor', 'Working in the factory' and 'Planting the trees in the countryside' – were fun but I was constantly in trouble for wanting to dance the army dance when it was time for the hoeing dance or for refusing to take the part of the landlord, the wolf, or the lazy-bones . . . During the next year, my second at the child-care center, I learned how to write my first characters. The first word was made up of the four strokes in [Chairman Mao's] name . . . during the third year and final fourth year at the child-care center we began our study properly, writing, 'Chairman Mao is our Great Saving Star', 'We are all

Chairman Mao's good little children'... 'When I am big I will be a worker' (or peasant or soldier) (Liang and Shapiro, 1983, p. 1).

Liang tells of his parents, his sisters and himself, living through periods of 'correction', away from home, becoming a Red Guard and eventually becoming a teacher in a middle school attached to a factory in Zhuzhou, where he concluded that the pupils were still being subjected to indoctrination, not taught how to evaluate events and actions for themselves. The fact that he himself emerged from his experiences a thinking human being and that he was inwardly questioning along the way, indicates that the system did not work, despite its early start. Of course, Liang's book does help us see and fight for the precious freedom to discuss ideas which may be counter to the prevailing ideology. The events in Tiananmen Square in 1989 bear further testimony to this spirit.

According to Rosen (1986), the period of world recession has coincided with greater levels of state funding for education in China. Although their level of investment is still behind that of most other nations, Rosen interprets this strategy as recognition that economic and educational development are interrelated. Rosen argues that those groups in China who disagree with this view of education as investment, seeing it rather as consumption and a drain on the economy, are not drawing this conclusion as a result of China's greater involvement in world affairs and thus, response to the recession, but as a result of earlier views of education, still widely held in the provinces, that education is consumer and welfare work.

Howard Reid's television documentary (BBC2 27.12.87) also focused on China. He suggested that with the possibility of childcare for all, women are able to pursue careers without appearing to be 'handicapped' by having a child. Meng Dai, a young mother and university professor, described her long working hours and her feelings of guilt at having sent her son to live with his grandparents on an island in the country, because she could spend so little time with him, even during the evenings. Reid explained that in China they are wary of opening more twenty-four-hour nurseries because of serious worries about the effects on the children. Reid argues that China offers a lesson to all societies where women are arguing for the provision of twenty-four-hour, or at least, day-long preschool facilities, since all over China, women are reported to be anxious about the conflict between bringing up children as one would wish and participating in the workforce. Such a documentary is interesting from the point of view that it provides us with the opportunity to empathize with women in another part of the world who are experiencing the same feelings Reid would have found in the UK. However, he appears to miss the point, made so often in arguments about availability for work, employment of women and the provision needed for their children – that women and men could share the childcare, that a system could be operated in the UK of concessions to families with young children which would allow them precious time to spend with the children who will be tomorrow's adults, as in Norway (Woodhead, 1979). Neustatter (1987) believes that China will resolve the problem of balancing the needs of the children with those of the parents before we in the UK have reached the stage of nation-wide nursery provision.

The care/education divide – do other countries suffer this dichotomy?

While we in the UK are making efforts to co-ordinate services for young children, but are still suffering the effects of the division due to care being seen as the domain of the DHSS and education the responsibility of the DES, what can we learn from the ways other countries organize provision?

The entry for the UK in the *International Year Book of Education* for 1980 (Unesco, 1980) mentions only nursery schools and nursery classes, and cites the ages of children attending these as ranging from two to five. In 1986 the government claimed (to howls of disbelieving protest) that 88 per cent of three- and four-year-olds attended some form of education or daycare (DES, 1986). Facilities for children under three years of age are scarce, catering for only just over 5 per cent of the preschool cohort, while Bone's (1977) survey found that such provision was sought by the parents of almost half of the under-threes.

Table 2 allows us to make some comparisons between levels of provision in the UK and that in some other European countries.

Table 2 Preschool provision in Europe. (Adapted from Moss, 1988). Figures relate to 1985 or 1986. In some cases the figures for two-year-olds are included with under-twos and are not given separately.

Country	Under-twos	2-year-olds	3- to 5-year olds
Belgium	20–25%	25%	95%
France	20–25%	50%	95%
Germany	3%	1.5%	74%
Italy	5%		88%
Netherlands	1–2%	25%	50%
UK	2%		44%

In provision seen as specifically *educational*, Belgium, the Netherlands and France outstripped the UK even when those children in reception classes were included in the UK's figures. Since 1975 statistics appear to show that the UK has improved this shortfall by increasing yet again the numbers of four-year-olds in reception classes in primary schools.

Ten years ago only three out of the twenty-two countries of the OECD operated their preschool facilities for children from birth to school age, with reference to a single government ministry. These were Iceland (Ministry of Education), Norway (Ministry of Consumer Affairs and Government Administration) and Sweden (Ministry of Health and Social Affairs). All the other countries placed the responsibility for children of three or four (in three countries children of age two) and over with an education ministry, with a preceeding or concurrent responsibility (that is from birth) with a welfare ministry. Thus, the UK is not alone in separating out the very young preschool children from those of three and four years old, or of having a daycare system for some of the older preschoolers not attending an educational establishment. It would appear that other nations, like the UK, lack

> a common philosophy about what services should be provided by whom and for whom, and with what overall aims. Despite well-intentioned reports, services remain low status and under-resourced, and the different histories and perspectives they embody tend to reinforce the existing divide between education and care (Pugh, 1988, p. 11).

Some examples of preschool provision

France

Despite the fact that the French are proud of their record of provision for preschool education – with nursery schools or nursery classes provided for 33.8 per cent of two-year-olds, 88 per cent of three-year-olds, and all four- and five-years-olds, according to Van der Eyken (1982) – in the report given by their ministerial representative to the Standing Conference in 1981 (Van der Eyken, 1982) indicated their concern for the staff–child ratios in some of their *écoles maternelles* (1 to 25 in classes of two-year-olds). However, the attention paid to this weakness, and the fact that preschool provision is an important electoral issue in France, were some indications that there was a political intention to rectify the situation. The study undertaken by Moss (1988) for the European Commission admits that data are sometimes difficult to produce or to use for comparisons. However, details of French provision indicate that approximately 20–25 per cent of children aged up to two years are in publicly funded services, and 95 per cent of those aged from three to five years are in pre-primary schooling, available for eight hours a day and with the possibility of school-based 'out-of-hours-care' facilities. There is also some limited tax relief on childcare costs for children up to age seven for home-based care facilities, whether that be in the child's or the carer's home, towards the social security payments of the carer.

France had already developed a system for supporting childminders by 1979, improving their status and training opportunities, and other daycare provision for the under-threes, in the form of day nurseries (*crèches collectives*) catering for over 39,000 children, with plans for 25,000 more places. There were also *haltes garderies*, offering short-term provision, and a few children's centres (*centres de la petite enfance*), which combined the other types of service. The representative to the 1981 Standing Conference (Van der Eyken, 1982) also emphasized the recognition, in France, of the need for education as the focus of provision. The aim is to develop the support given to families, so that parents are aware that, from the earliest days of life, they are the first educators. This idea of flexible support for the family, together with President Mitterrand's announced intention that there would be universal nursery provision for all children over the age of two within a few years, makes the UK record appear somewhat feeble. It is no wonder that when it was the turn of the UK representative to speak, stress was placed, somewhat defensively, on the fact that 'education for children of this age in the UK is not a child-minding service designed to enable parents to go out to work' (Van der Eyken, 1982, p. 146). Such a statement could indeed have been interpreted by other delegates as implying that their efforts to provide educational experiences for young children were being denigrated by the representative of a country with an extemely poor record.

Deasey (1978), following a visit to a typical *école maternelle*, with its silent, formal interiors and carefully ordered day, asks his readers not to judge with Anglo-Saxon values. He writes of the French care with appearance (thus, children must stay neat), the respect among all classes for in-tellectual achievement and the belief that happiness is dependent upon a well-regulated and self-controlled life. He also adds that the *directrice* of the *maternelle* he visited had forty-five of '*les grands*' in a class she taught single-handed. The *directrice* apologized for the fact that, although there were moves to develop more progressive methods, she felt she lacked the training and confidence to change to freer activities. The day lasts from 7.50 a.m. to 4.30 p.m. and there are regulations governing the order of activities allowed. Physical movement must intervene between bouts of intellectual activity and concentration, but even the manual work and physical activity are strongly directed.

New Zealand

Most of New Zealand's preschool population attend some form of group provision. Although there have recently been attempts to co-ordinate different services, by integrating the administration under one government department, Education, leaving only the Maori *kohanga reo* (developed in 1982 to preserve Maori language and culture), to be funded by the Department of Maori Affairs, Smith (1987) claims that some of the problems arise because provision is made as part of a reactive, rather than a proactive, process. The New Zealand Minister of Education in 1985, Marshall, in an address, made the point that provision is only made in response to need articulated by parents seeking what they deem best for their children. Sensitivity to the needs of children whose parents are unable to articulate their wishes in as forceful a way as the case may demand are then clearly at a disadvantage.

There are four main types of early childhood services in New Zealand. *Kingdergartens* provide sessional education, five mornings a week for four-year-olds, and on three afternoons for three-year-olds. Teachers (with two years' training) work with groups of up to forty children and there is a ratio of one teacher to twenty children. Although kindergarten is free, parents will often make donations equivalent to up to £2 per week. The kindergarten movement began in Dunedin in 1889, it now caters for over half the population of preschool attenders and receives the largest proportion of government funding. The kindergarten philosophy is based on Froebelian ideas.

Although *playcentres* began during the Second World War as support groups for mothers whose husbands were away, they are very like UK playgroups. They offer children aged two-and-a-half to five play provision within a group of twenty children, run by a supervisor who receives an honorarium, not a salary, assisted by a rota of parents. Playcentres provide for about a fifth of three- and four-year-olds. They are helped with the costs of equipment, premises and training by government grants, although these amount to only about 8 per cent of funding provided for the kindergartens.

Nga kohanga reo (Maori language nests) were begun in 1982 with one centre and by 1987 there were estimated to be well over 450 such centres, catering for 10 per cent of under-fives, probably around 8,000 children. Since the main aim of these centres is the promotion of Maori culture and language, children may attend from birth and the system is organized flexibly, being run by older Maori-speaking women. Again, the provision receives government funding, in this case amounting to approximately one-third of the amount received by the kindergarten system.

Childcare is the generic name given to all other types of preschool provision in New Zealand not included in the three systems already described. Groups such as private nurseries, community kingdergartens, private kindergartens, some with flexible hours, some catering for the younger children, others for those over two-and-a-half years old, shoppers' crèches, Steiner and Montessori schools, and so on, come into this category. About one fifth of the under fives are found in these varied forms of provision. Just as such provision would be under the DHSS umbrella in Britain, the childcare centres were administered by the Department of Social Welfare in New Zealand.

In 1986 the childcare centres were, with all the other forms of provision, transferred to the Department of Education. Countries like the UK may find much to be learnt from their experiences, since they, too, live in a society where attitudes to motherhood and the provision of facilities for young children outside the home have hampered the development of anything which enables parents to leave their children for more than a few hours a day. Smith (1987) states that the costs of childcare centre places, despite the poor salaries paid to staff, are too high for many of the poorer families who need day care so that they can work. These parents are resorting to childminders, a group whose organization in New Zealand appears to lag in development compared with their UK counterparts. There, no regulations exist to cover the quality, number, cost and planning of places with childminders.

A further anxiety expressed in Smith's study of provision in New Zealand is the possibility of the introduction of a voucher system for education. She feels that such a system would have disastrous effects on the lower-income families, who would elect to use their vouchers to buy 'the cheapest and probably the lowest quality service'.

Many of the issues surrounding the situation in New Zealand are similar to those currently on the agenda in the UK, issues such as the status of staff, co-operation between services, relations with parents and the need for increased funding to encourage better-quality centres.

Japan

Japan is much mentioned in press reports which claim that UK school-leavers' standards of achievement are lower than those achieved in other countries, and that, as a result, the UK economy is failing to compete adequately with those of other countries. While 94 per cent of Japan's school-leavers (over-15s) continue their education voluntarily, only about half of Britain's post-16-year-olds choose to stay on. Similarly while only one in seven of Britons aged 18–22 goes to university, more than one in three of Japan's cohort does so (Lynn, 1988).

Does such motivation begin during the early years of life in Japan? Certainly, Japanese parents have to set their children in pursuit of academic excellence very early in life if they are to proceed onto the next rung in the very competitive ladder to success in adulthood.

Japan has both state and private preschool provision. Approximately 25 per cent is maintained. The private kindergartens charge fees which make up about one-third of their income, the rest being made up of a government subsidy and funding from endowments and loans. Parents also pay small fees for state kindergarten attendance. Some 85 per cent of children over three attend kindergarten, until entering school at six. In kindergarten the children are expected to learn to read and to carry out simple addition and subtraction calculations, although Japanese mothers are keen to develop their children's academic abilities at home, too. In the kindergarten there is less emphasis on play than in UK nurseries, but there are activities to promote the children's skills of thinking, observation, learning and general intelligence (Lynn, 1988). Because the education system in Japan is highly selective, mothers seeking places for their children at the 'top' private kindergarten are themselves given intelligence tests, as are the children. The mothers are tested because of the high correlation between mothers' IQ scores and those of offspring. Lynn argues that the willingness of parents including those in lower-income and working-class groups, to pay quite substantial fees for preschool provision, is a mark of Japanese commitment to their children's education. Lynn's remark, if intended to be comparative, may be a little unfair, however, since Japanese colleagues inform me that these fees are approximately equivalent to a British playgroup place three sessions per week.

Back to the UK

The form preschool provision should take, especially where a nation decides that such provision should be termed 'educational', is likely to vary depending on a number of factors, one of which will be the outcomes desired by that society. Even within Japan there is debate about whether kindergarten should be formal or play-orientated, and there is a proliferation of curricula, some predominantly musical, others sport-orientated, for example (personal communication from Professor

Mitsuhiro Yonetani). The evidence provided by research (see, for example Jowett and Sylva, 1986) to suggest that guided play provides children with cognitive challenge and activities which match children's abilities, particularly when adults intervene in a collaborative way with the children, leads one to support such a model in a democratic society whose members place a high value on liberty, equality and fraternity (which I would prefer to call 'solidarity'). Children in a guided play setting are exercising choice and making independent decisions, but they are also required to realize that their decisions may interfere with the freedom of others, so they learn about responsibility, too. Where staff are aware of potential prejudice, children are afforded equality of opportunity, and the solidarity comes from the enjoyment of sharing chosen activities with others, both during the task and at the review stage. The way in which our society actually provides opportunities for those experiences for all our children is another matter, dependent on political decisions, the economy, cultural and ideological factors.

In the UK we have experienced the effects of the recession more harshly than, for example, Japanese society, and one of the effects of a recession can be a reforming of old ranks, a revival of conflicts in society which in boom years are submerged. Wirt and Harmann (1986) argue that this is most likely to occur when the recession is caused by events outside a nation's control, so that privileged groups and their education are protected. Add to this idea the implementation of a more investment-oriented and instrumental education system, with abandonment of a liberal curriculum, and one wonders if we will see a rise in the number of private, academically-focused preschool establishments in the UK. Although experts like Professor Lilian Katz have warned of cramming causing 'burnout' by five (*Times Educational Supplement*, 18 September 1987), there are already reports of 5 per cent increases in private sector nursery classes. In her report to the European Commission, Goutard (1980) described what she was already witnessing of a movement towards training rather than education. She called for greater awareness of the threat such instrumentalism poses to children's freedom.

CONCLUSIONS

13
Towards educare?

The opportunity for parents to demand adequate provision of high-quality care facilities, currently a priority topic on the agendas of both government and employers, may not occur again in quite the same way as it has now, at the beginning of the 1990s. Allied to the recognition that demographic change will mean a demand for women's membership of the labour force in even greater proportions than those previously encountered in the United Kindom, there is a parallel recognition that many women with young children work outside the home only when driven by economic circumstances. Others, despite dreams of combining an exciting, full-time career with a family (Riach, 1989), find the reality all too depressing (Fogarty *et al.*, 1981). A combination of the wish to be available to children when they are small, to share their lives and experiences, and a dissatisfaction with either the levels or the quality of care provision, and anxiety about the way they themselves are perceived by many work colleagues and superiors, makes the struggle unattractive. If they could be sure that they would be valued for their expertise and experiences, respected as guardians of future citizens, and therefore allowed to work flexible hours without any loss of career status, with leave for children's illnesses for both parents, and, perhaps most importantly, if high-quality child-care combined with education – in other words, educare – were easily available, then possibly even those not forced to do so would be more willing to participate in economic activity. Furthermore, an amelioration in the conditions of the growing numbers of women whose earnings are an essential part of the family's basic income would better equip them to perform their various roles. This is also a time at which, with the implementation of a National Curriculum, the government is aiming to improve standards of achievement in schools for 5–16-year-olds, but this will be a difficult task if children under five have not experienced learning opportunities which foster their cognitive growth and enable them to meet new challenges with joy, curiosity and confidence.

Investing in the future?

The value of nursery education for children under five is endorsed by the government in *Better Schools* (DES, 1985, pp. 38–40):

> Nearly all children stand to benefit from some attendance at school before reaching the compulsory age provided that what the school offers is appropriate to their age and stage of development...The education of young children is founded on play...The Government has encouraged the education and the social services departments of local authorities to develop coordination between the provision of education and care for under fives.

We will require research into the long-term effects of different forms, regimes, levels of staffing, and so on, of preschool experience.

A report by one of the Conservative government think tanks, the Adam Smith Institute (1989), suggests that there is a great deal of money to be made out of the provision of preschool facilities, near stations, workplaces, and so on. The question is whether the nation should be thinking about investing in the future by providing good, well-regulated educational provision as a foundation for the National Curriculum – in other words, investing in the whole future citizenry – or whether a few entrepreneurs should be allowed to invest capital in order to make profits out of small children and their parents, and with little guarantee that the children will be receiving a combination of care and *education*. Hughes *et al.* (1980) demonstrated that any form of high-quality provision will be as costly as LEA nursery education.

This is a question of values, a debate about the underpinning philosophy and beliefs by which people live. Other questions will need to be addressed during the 1990s, and there will probably be changes in the way of life of some of the population, which will lead to further questions relating to preschool provision. I have attempted to address some of those issues in this book but events will doubtless occur which will change the lives of young children and their parents, and those of workers in the preschool field, in ways which are difficult to predict, so that some questions are left unanswered.

Possible changes in family life

With the current speed of technological developments, is it possible that an increasing number of parents will be enabled to spend part of their working week based at home? We do not yet know how great this movement may be, nor its effects on families, but it is possible that this type of change, combined with growing awareness about environmental issues and conservation, may lead to greater numbers of parents, both men and women, deciding to work shorter hours, or to choose work they can carry out, for the most part, in their homes. Such parents are likely to want very flexible facilities, close to home, but still with support, which means that while they are working, their children are happy and experiencing the kinds of curricula they would choose.

Parental worries about preschool provision

The wish to offer parents the choice between a particular type of provision for their under-fives and keeping them at home may be laudable. But how *real* is the element of choice? Choice based on market forces means that those who can afford to pay most have the greatest choice. For some there will still be little choice. Working-class women lucky enough to find that their employer operates a workplace crèche, or contracts local childminders, will not only be forced to take their children with them to the locality in which they work, but will also, under current tax regulations, be required to pay tax on the 'perk' of this facility. Further, they are the group most likely to change employment, or to be in and out of work at fairly regular intervals, so that the care arrangements for their children are also likely to change frequently.

As certain groups of parents become better informed about the National Curriculum for 5–16-year-olds, and the way in which progress is to be assessed, will they demand high-quality provision which offers continuity of experience for their children? Because many parents will be anxious to ensure that their children do not lose out during their earliest years, they will wish to become well informed about early learning. If the children are in provision offering them activities which foster exploration and first-hand experience through play, and opportunities to reflect on those experiences, with other children and adults, they will be gaining a firm foundation. Parents will expect staff to be able to explain to them why certain practices occur and, most particularly, what the benefits will be to their children. It is difficult to see how children attending for only a few sessions per week will learn from experiences lacking in continuity, or that children can benefit in groups so large, in comparison with the number of qualified staff, that they receive inadequate attention.

Parents who have employed a minder or a nanny, or whose children have attended some form of full-day care, may be reluctant to move them to a nursery school or class which does not offer extended hours.

For very young children, some parents will perhaps be wary of institutional facilities. Mortimore and Mortimore (1985) addressed the issue of whether group provision might be benign or malignant and came to the conclusion that this was not dependent upon the institution having a particular function, it was more to do with the organization, philosophy and ethos – which in turn depended upon the willingness of staff to be self-evaluative; to de-centre and examine their establishment from the children's point of view; to change their own attitudes, particularly those relating to parents and other professionals; and to recognize the importance of home–group relations.

Staffing educare facilities

At the outset of the 1990s as demographic changes begin to bite, will there be enough early years teachers to sustain an educational input into preschool provision? Although the statistics show that there is no shortage of people qualified as teachers in the UK, schools in many areas are experiencing difficulty in recruiting staff, because qualified teachers are moving into other professions owing to the malaise in their own. There has been a doubling of this effect on nurseries because, first as in other sectors, there is a shortage of early years teachers applying for posts (in fact there is a shortage of training places because many colleges specializing in early years work were closed in the 1970s), and second, some of those already in nursery teaching positions have been moved into primary school vacancies in the statutory sector. This appears to be a reiteration by society of the relative importance placed on compulsory education compared with the preschool years.

The disenchantment causing the shortages is said to be the result of low pay and morale in the teaching profession. It is also claimed that the speed with which all the changes emanating from the Education Reform Act are expected to be implemented is exhausting the profession both physically and emotionally. Although nursery teachers have been to some extent excluded from these arrangements, they are none the less required to know and understand all the documents and to appreciate potential effects on their own sector.

If salary levels are not increased it will be difficult to attract workers from the dramatically reduced labour force into teaching in general, and early years education in particular, where promotion prospects are traditionally poor, despite high levels of commitment from those who choose to work with this age-group.

A further aspect of morale, status and pay which will affect the possibility of continuity for children, and which will require monitoring in the years ahead, will be the stability, or otherwise, of staffing in preschool provision. If the labour shortage is as severe as predicted, all preschool workers will be reluctant to stay in employment for which they feel they are inadequately paid and for which they are accorded low status by society. Frequent changes of staffing will not be beneficial to young children. It is all very well to insist that caring staff will put the children first, but staff who feel themselves to be undervalued or underpaid will not stay long – or, if they do, they will leak their misery into the group. One important aspect of good provision for young children will be the contentedness and thus the continuity of its staff members.

The recruitment of teachers from the European Community will have particular relevance for early years work, since under-fives professionals with teacher training qualifications obtained in the UK are an important group in maintaining the credibility of nursery professionalism. It is their accepted expertise and the opportunity to move into, and out of, the primary school phase which is vital. We do not yet know what effect the opening of our school doors to those with European qualifications will have on the nurseries. In France, for example, nursery teachers receive only two years' training, whereas in the UK they receive four years' education after A level, so that they have a degree and teaching qualification at the end of those four years. (It must also be remembered that the UK's statutory school entry age of five is lower than that of the other European countries. Again using France as the example, five-year-olds in France are taught by those with only two years' training.)

Various factors have influenced the relative absence of men, members of minority ethnic groups, especially Afro-Caribbeans and Asians, and those with ambition for their career development, from the ranks of early childhood professionals. The pay, status and gender stereotyping of the work have led to the discouragement of male representation; institutional racism, coupled with unhappy educational experiences and few enticements to become teachers, have probably led to the low numbers of minority group teachers. Parallel prejudice has ensured that most early years teachers tend to be white, unassertive young women, often regarding themselves as not particularly clever – a view they often had confirmed in their interactions with others. As the education of young children is in fact as complex as, if not more complex than, that of older groups, we need to destroy this myth, along with the other social prohibitions. We need articulate and committed teachers from all groups to work with young children at a time when they are most open, most receptive and most vulnerable.

In order to ensure that children experience high-quality care facilities in which education is embedded, it is vital that the most appropriate use be made of the expertise of the early years teachers and advisers who are recruited. There may need to be an expansion in these posts. Following this, as part of developments in the near future, workers in different facilities for under-fives and their families are likely to be asked to collaborate more closely together, and in some areas this has already been the case for some time. If additional teachers and advisers are employed by local authorities to help develop the curriculum in 'satellite' bases, careful planning and monitoring on the part of other staff, for example, playgroup supervisors, daycare staff, local childminders, and also by parents with children at home, will be important. It would be easy to minimize the difficulties faced by workers trying to achieve this co-operation and co-ordination. As Pugh and De'Ath (1989) have stated, the fact that there are only around forty combined nursery centres in the UK bears testimony to the challenges of bringing differently trained workers, with different aims and objectives, different pay and career structures, together. Staff may need support and training, as well as opportunities to discuss any real or perceived grievances. Watt (1977) found that teaching staff tended to cause distress among other professionals and volunteers, due to the invisible barriers they erected to protect their own professionalism. Early years teachers, together with others, need time and training if they are to achieve the kind of relationships needed to make co-ordinated under-fives provision work. We need to carry out research into the ways co-operation can be fostered, the kinds of courses which promote positive relationships between groups of workers and the range of support they require.

To complicate the issue further, there are those who fear that if teachers of under-fives are brought into a closely-knit pre-fives organization, they will lose their identities as teachers and the close links they share with colleagues in the statutory sector. Again, this is something for which time will need to be allowed, because continuity with the statutory sector will be essential if the National Curriculum is to be a success.

What complications may arise from the new concept of local financial management of schools relating to provision for our youngest children? Some school governing bodies are realizing that their budgets will be insufficient to cover the salaries of some of their experienced teachers. By reclassifying a nursery class as a school playgroup, the governors could cease to employ a teacher in that class. This would be an unwise move for a school hoping to give its under-fives a firm foundation for the National Curriculum, but in an ethos of misunderstanding about the nature of nursery education and learning through play, it is a decision which many could erroneously take. Early childhood educators need to develop public relations skills so as to inform school governors, parents, colleagues in voluntary and other care sectors, and the community, about their work.

Keeping children at the centre of our concerns

How can we foster continuity of experience which will benefit children? The importance of continuity and co-ordination in children's early experiences is stressed in many of the research reports cited in this book. It is also likely to be related to the style of learning of the children involved, for, as Bloom (1964) pointed out, a child's learning style at age three is likely to be the style displayed at age six, and one wonders if this style is usually adopted for life as a consequence. Children who are moved from one facility to another, or whose carers do not take time to liaise with each other fully, may experience discontinuities and stress which limit their future capacity for learning. We therefore need to monitor which groups in society are most likely to be involved, the experiences of those children vulnerable to changes of carer or group, and the resultant effects.

Children themselves often seem to be forgotten when the economy or the needs of industry are being debated, yet we observe over and over again that a society which takes account of its most vulnerable members understands that what happens to young children in the here and now will have repercussions in the future. Young children deserve the best we can give them now, as a human right. For the present and for the future we must work to ensure that all our under-fives are appropriately educated.

Bibliography

Adam Smith Institute (1989) *Mind the children*. London, Adam Smith Institute.

AFFOR (1983) *Issues and resources*. Birmingham, AFFOR.

Ainsworth, M. (1973) 'The development of infant–mother attachment' in B. Caldwell (ed.), *Review of child development research*, Vol. 3, Chicago, University of Chicago Press.

Ainsworth, M., Bell, S.M. and Stayton, D.J. (1974) 'Infant-mother attachment and social development' in M.P.M. Richards (ed.), *The integration of the child into the social world*. Cambridge, Cambridge University Press.

Alexander, R. (1988) 'Garden or jungle? Teacher development and informal primary education' in A. Blyth (ed.), *Informal primary education today*. London, Falmer.

Alexander, R. (1989) 'Core subjects and Autumn leaves: the National Curriculum and the language of Primary education', *Education 3–13*, 17, 1, 3–8.

Al-Khalifa, E. (1988) 'Pin money professional? Women in teaching' in A. Coyle and J. Skinner (eds), *Women and work*. London, Macmillan Education.

Allen, S. (1976) 'Pre-school children: ethnic minorities in England', *New Community*, 7, 2, 135–42.

Archer, J. (1989) 'Childhood gender roles: structure and development', *The Psychologist*, 2, 9, 363–6.

Archer, J. and Lloyd, B. (1985) *Sex and gender*. Cambridge, Cambridge University Press.

Aries, P. (1962) *Centuries of childhood*. London, Jonathan Cape.

Atkin, J. and Webb, J. (1985) *Nursery education: a study guide*. Nottingham, University of Nottingham, School of Education.

Austen, R., Cross, M. and Johnson, M. (1984) *Unequal and under five: a background paper on ethnic minority under fives*. Warwick, Centre for Research in Ethnic Relations, Warwick University/VOLCUF.

BAECE and PPA (1987) *Four years old but not yet five. A Joint Statement*. London, BAECE/PPA.

Barrett, G. (1986) *Starting school: an evaluation of the experience.* London, Assistant Masters and Mistresses Association.

Bate, M., Smith, M., Sumner, R. and Sexton, B. (1978) *Manual for assessment in nursery education.* Windsor, NFER-Nelson.

Bathurst, K. (1905) 'Report of women inspectors on children under five years of age in elementary schools' in W. Van der Eyken (ed.) (1975) *Education, the child and society: a documentary history, 1900–1973.* Harmondsworth, Penguin.

Beechey, V (1986) 'Studies of women's employment' in Feminist Review (eds), *Waged work.* London, Virago.

Beechey, V. and Perkins, T. (1987) *A matter of hours, women, part-time work and the labour market.* Cambridge, Polity Press.

Belotti, E.G. (1975) *Little Girls.* London, Writers and Readers.

Bennett, D. (1987) 'The aims of teachers and parents for children in their first year of school' in NFER/SCDC Seminar Report, *Four year olds in school.* Slough, NFER/SCDC.

Bennett, N. (1976) *Teaching style and pupil progress.* London, Open Books.

Bennett, N. and Kell, J. (1989) *A good start?* Oxford, Blackwell.

Bernstein, B. (1975) *Class, codes and control.* London, Routledge and Kegan Paul.

Bernstein, B. (1977) 'Class and pedagogies: visible and invisible' in A. Karabel and A.H. Halsey (eds), *Power and ideology in education.* Oxford, Oxford University Press.

Berruetta-Clement, J.R., Schwinhart, L.J., Barnett, W.S., Epstein, A. and Weikart, D.P. (1984) *Changed lives: the effects of the Perry Pre-school Program on youth through age 19 years.* Ypsilanti MI, High Scope Press Monograph.

Beveridge, M. and Dunn, J. (1980) 'Communication and the development of reflective thinking', paper presented at the BPS Conference (Developmental Section), University of Edinburgh.

Blackstone, T. (1971) *A fair start.* London, Allen Lane.

Blackstone, T. (1988) 'Positive discrimination and education', public lecture, University of Warwick, January.

Blatchford, P., Battle, S. and Mays, J. (1982) *The first transition.* Windsor, NFER-Nelson.

Blenkin, G.M. and Kelly, A.V. (1987) *Early childhood education: a developmental curriculum.* London, Paul Chapman.

Block, J. (1984) *Sex role identity and ego developments.* San Fransisco, Jossey-Bass.

Bloom, B.S. (1964) *Stability and change in human characteristics.* New York, Wiley.

Blyth, A. (ed.) (1988) *Informal primary education today.* London, Falmer.

Board of Education (1943) *White paper on education.* London, HMSO.

Boh, K., Bak, M., Clason, C., Pankratova, M., Qvortup, J., Sgritta, G.B. and Waerness, K. (1989) *Changing patterns of European family life.* London, Routledge.

Bone, M. (1977) *Preschool children and the need for daycare* (DHSS Survey). London, HMSO.

Bowlby, J. (1951) *Maternal care and mental health.* Geneva, World Health Organisation.

Bowlby, J. (1953) *Child care and the growth of love.* Harmondsworth, Penguin.

Bowlby, J. (1969) *Attachment and loss. Vol. 1: Attachment.* Hogarth Press.

Bradley, M. (1982) *The coordination of services for children under five.* Windsor, NFER-Nelson.

Brannen, J. and Moss, P. (1988) *New mothers at work.* London,Unwin Hyman.

Brierley, J. (1984) *Give me a child until he is seven. Brain studies and early childhood education.* London, Falmer.

Bronfenbrenner, U. (1977) 'Towards an experimental ecology of human development', *American Psychologist*, 32, 513–31.

Bronfenbrenner, U. (1979) *The ecology of human development.* Cambridge, MA, Harvard University Press.

Brown, A.L. (1977) 'Development, schooling and the acquisition of knowledge about knowledge' in R.C. Anderson, R.J. Shapiro and W.E. Montague (eds), *Schooling and the acquisition of knowledge.* Hillsdale, NJ, Erlbaum.

Brown, G., Bholchrain, M. and Harris, T.D. (1975) 'Social class and psychiatric disturbance among women in an urban population', *Sociology*, 9, 225–54.

Brown, G. and Harris, T. D. (1978) *Social origins of depression: a study of psychiatric disorder in women.* London, Tavistock.

Brown, N. and France, P. (eds) (1986) *Untying the apron strings.* Milton Keynes, Open University Press.

Bruce, T. (1987) *Early childhood education.* London, Hodder and Stoughton.

Bruner, J. (1980) *Under five in Britain.* London, Grant McIntyre.

Bruner, J. (1984) 'Vygotsky's zone of proximal development: the hidden agenda' in B. Rogoff and J.V. Wertsch (eds), *Children's learning in the 'zone of proximal development'.* San Francisco, Jossey-Bass.

Bruner, J. (1986) 'On teaching thinking: an afterthought' in S.F. Chipman, J.W. Segal and R. Glaser (eds), *Thinking and learning skills: research and open questions.* Hillsdale, NJ. Erlbaum.

Bruner, J.S. (1977) *The process of instruction.* Cambridge, MA, Harvard University Press.

Bryans, T. (1987) 'Curriculum for under fives: from principles to practice', paper presented to NCB Seminar, London, 3 June.

Bryant, B., Harris, M. and Newton, D. (1980) *Children and minders.* London, Grant McIntyre.

CACE (1967) *Children and their primary schools* (Plowden Report). London, HMSO.

Campbell, R.J., Coates, E., David, T., Fitzgerald, J., Goodyear, R., Jowett, M., Lewis, A., Neil, S. St J. and Sylva, K. (1990) *Assessing 3- to 8-year-olds.* Windsor, NFER.

Campos, J.J., Barrett, K.C., Lamb, M.E., Goldsmith, H.H. and Sternberg, C. (1983) 'Socio-emotional development' in M.M. Haith and J.J. Campos (eds), *Handbook of Child Development*, Vol. 2, New York, Wiley.

Carby, H. (1980) *Multicultural fictions.* Occasional stencilled paper no 58. Centre for Contemporary Cultural Studies, University of Birmingham.

Cass, J.E. (1975) *The role of the teacher in the nursery school.* Oxford, Pergamon.

Central Policy Review Staff (1979) *Services for young children with working mothers.* London: HMSO.

CERI (1982) *Caring for children.* Paris, OECD.

Chapman, N. (1989) 'Swings and sensibilities', *Guardian* 17 June.

Child Education (1986) 'Minister's line on primaries', *Child Education*, December.

Christie, J.F. (1986) 'Training in symbolic play' in P.K. Smith (ed.), *Children's play: research developments and practical applications.* New York, Gordon and Breach.

City of Sheffield (1986) *Nursery education: guidelines for curriculum organisation and assessment.* Sheffield, Education Media Centre.

Clark, K. and Clark, M. (1947) 'Racial identification and preference in negro children' in T.N. Newcomb and E.L. Hartley (eds), *Readings in Social Psychology.* New York, Holt.

Clark, M.M. (1983) 'Early education; issues and evidence', *Educational Review*, 35, 2, 113–20.

Clark, M.M. (1988) *Children under five: educational research and evidence.* London, Gordon and Breach.

Clark, M.M., Barr, J.E. and Dewhirst, W. (1984) 'Early education of children with communication problems: particularly those from ethnic minorities', DES-funded research report, Birmingham University.

Clarke, A.M. and Clarke, A.D.B. (eds) (1976) *Early experience: myth and evidence.* London, Open Books.

Clarke-Stewart, A. (1982) *Day care.* London, Fontana.

Clarke-Stewart, A. and Fein, G.G. (1983) 'Early childhood programs' in M.M. Haith and J.J. Campos (eds), *Handbook of child psychology*, Vol. 2. New York, Wiley.

Clarricoates, K. (1978) 'Dinosaurs in the clasroom – a re-examination of some aspects of the hidden curriculum in primary schools', *Women's Studies International Quarterly*, 1, 4, 353–64.

Cleave, S., Jowett, S. and Bate, M. (1982) *And so to school.* Windsor, NFER-Nelson.

Clift, P., Cleave, S. and Griffin, M. (1980) *The aims, role and deployment of staff in the nursery.* Windsor, NFER.

Coard, B. (1971) *How the West Indian child is made educationally subnormal in the British school system.* London, New Beacon Books.

Cochran, M. (1986) 'The parental empowerment process building on family strengths' in J. Harris (ed.) *Child Psychology in Action.* London, Croom Helm.

Cockburn, C. (1989) 'Second among equals', *Marxism Today*, July.

Cohen, B. (1988) *Caring for children: services and policies for childcare and equal opportunties in the United Kingdom.* London, Commission of the European Communities.

Committee on Child Health Services (1976) *Fit for the future* (Court Report), Cmnd 6684. London, HMSO.

Consultative Committee (1933) *Report on infant and nursery schools* (Hadow Report). London, HMSO.

Corbishley, H. (1984) 'Linking professionals, voluntary organisations and parents' in G. Pugh and E. De'Ath (eds), *Partnership papers 1: Working together, parents and professionals as partners.* London, NCB.

CPAG (1987) *Poverty: the facts.* London, CPAG.

CRC (1975) *Who minds?* London, CRC.

CRE (1977) *Caring for under-fives in a multi-racial society.* London, CRE.

CRE (1987) 'Report special – education to meet the needs and reflect the nature of its multicultural society', *New Equals*, 27, 10.

Crocker, A.C. and Cheeseman, R.G. (1988) 'Infant teachers have a major impact on children's self-awareness', *Children and Society*, 2, 1, 3–8.

Cummins, J. (1976) 'The influence of bilingualism on cognitive growth', *Working papers on bilingualism*, 9, April.

Cunningham, C. and Davis, H. (1985) *Working with parents*. Milton Keynes, Open University Press.

Curtis, A. (1986) *A curriculum for the preschool child*. Windsor, NFER-Nelson.

Curtis, A. and Hill, S. (1978) *My world: a handbook of ideas*. Windsor, NFER-Nelson.

Cyster, R., Clift, P.S. and Battles, S. (1980) *Parental Involvement in Primary Schools*, Windsor, NFER.

Dansky, J.L. and Silverman, I.W. (1973) 'Effects of play on associative fluency', *Developmental Psychology*, 9, 38–43.

David, M.E. (1980) *The state, the family and education*. London, Routledge and Kegan Paul.

David, T. and Lewis, A. (1989) 'Assessment in the reception class' in L. Harding and J. Beech (eds), *Assessment in the primary school*. Windsor, NFER.

Davie, C., Hutt, S.J., Vincent, E. and Mason, M (1984) *The young child at home*. Windsor, NFER-Nelson.

Davie, R., Butler, N. and Goldstein, H. (1972) *From birth to seven*. London, Longman.

Davies, B. (1987) 'The accomplishment of genderedness in pre-school children' in A. Pollard (ed.), *Children and their primary schools*. London, Falmer.

Deasey, D. (1978) *Education under six*. London, Croom Helm.

Deem, R. (1986) 'Gender and social class' in R. Rogers (ed.). *Education and social class*. London, Falmer.

DES (1963) *Half our future* (Newsom Report). London, HMSO.

DES (1964) *Addendum No. 1. to Circular 8/60*. (7 July 1964, par. 2.) London, HMSO.

DES (1972) *Education: a framework for expansion*. Education White Paper, Cmnd. 5174. London, HMSO.

DES (1975) *A language for life* (Bullock Report). London, HMSO.

DES (1977) *A new partnership for our schools* (Taylor Report). London, HMSO.

DES (1978a) *Primary education in England: A survey by HM Inspectors of schools*. London, HMSO.

DES (1978b) *Report of the Committee of Enquiry into the education of handicapped children and young people* (Warnock Report). London, HMSO.

DES (1981a) *West Indian children in our schools* (Rampton Report). London, HMSO.

DES (1981b) *The school curriculum*. London, HMSO.

DES (1982) *Education 5 to 9: an illustrative survey of 80 first schools in England*. London, HMSO.

DES (1985a) *Curriculum matters 2: Curriculum 5–16* (HMI discussion document). London, HMSO.

DES (1985b) *Education for all* Swann Report). London, HMSO.

DES (1985c) *Better schools*. London, HMSO.

DES (1986) *Statistical Bulletin*, 16/86. London, HMSO.

DES (1987) *The National Curriculum 5-16: a consultation doucument*. London, HMSO.

DES (1988a) *Combined provision for the under fives: the contribution of education* (HMI report). London, HMSO.

DES (1988b) *National Curriculum: Science for ages 5-16*. London, HMSO.

DES (1988c) *National Curiculum Task Group on Assessment and Testing. A report*. London, HMSO.

DES (1989) *Aspects of primary education. The education of children under five*. London, HMSO.

Desforges, C. (1989) 'Labelling traps we must avoid', *Times Educational Supplement*, 26 May, p. A18.

Desforges, C. and Cockburn, A. (1987) *Understanding the mathematics teacher*. London, Falmer.

Development Education Centre (1984) *Starting together*. Birmingham, DEC.

Dewey, J. (1933) *How we Think: a Restatement of the Relation of Reflective Thinking to the Educative Process*. Chicago, Henry Regnery.

Dex, S. (1985) *The sexual division of work*. Brighton, Wheatsheaf Books.

Dex, S. (1988) *Women's attitudes towards work*. London, Macmillan.

DHSS and DES (1976) *Low cost day provision for the under-fives*. London, HMSO.

Doise, W. and Mugny, G. (1984) *The social development of the intellect*. Oxford, Pergamon.

Donaldson, M. (1978) *Children's minds*. Glasgow, Fontana.

Donaldson, M. (1982) 'Conservation: what is the question?' *British Journal of Psychology*, 73, 199-207.

Douglas, J.W.B. (1964) *The home and the schools*. London, MacGibbon and Kee.

Douglas, J.W.B. and Ross, J.M. (1965) 'The later educational progress and emotional adjustment of children who went to nursery schools or classes.' *Educational Research*, 7, 2, 73-80.

Dowling, M. (1988) *Education 3 to 5: a teachers' handbook*. London, Paul Chapman.

Dunn, J. (1987) 'Understanding feelings: the early stages' in J. Bruner and H. Haste (eds), *Making sense*. London, Methuen.

Dye, J. (1984) 'Early education matters. A study of preschool curriculum content', *Educational Research*, 26, 95-105.

Ebbeck, M. (1985) 'Teachers' behaviours towards boys and girls', *OMEP Update*, 6, October.

Edwards, D. and Mercer, N. (1987) *Common knowledge*. London, Methuen.

Edwards, V. (1986) *Language in a black community*. Clevendon, Avon, Multilingual Matters.

Eisenstadt, N. (1985) 'Sharing management' in G. Pugh and E. De'Ath (eds), *Partnership papers 2*. London, NCB.

Eggleston, J., Dunn, D. and Anjali, M. (1986) *Education for some*. Stoke-on-Trent, Trentham Books.

Elliott, N. (1989) 'An overview of the conference.' National Primary Conference, March 1989, Scarborough.

EOC (1982) *An equal start*. Manchester, EOC.

EOC (1988) *Women and men in Britain*. London, HMSO.

160 *Bibliography*

Etaught, C. (1974) 'Effects of maternal employment on children: a review of recent research', *Merrill-Palmer Quarterly*, 20, 71–98.

Family Policy Studies Centre (1989) *Children under five: Fact sheet 7*. London, FPSC.

Ferri, E., Birchall, D., Gingell, V. and Gipps, C. (1981) *Combined nursery centres*. London, Macmillan.

Field, F. (1974) *Unequal Britain*. London, Arrow Books.

Fogarty, M.P., Allen, I. and Walters, P. (1981) *Women in top jobs*. London, Heinemann.

Fonda, N. and Moss, P. (eds) (1976) *Mothers in employment*. London, Brunel University Management Programme/Thomas Coram Res. Unit.

French, J. and French, P. (1984) 'Gender imbalance in the primary classroom: an interactional account', *Educational Research*, 26, 2.

Garland, C. and White, S. (1980) *Children and day nurseries*. London, Grant McIntyre.

Garvey, C. (1977) *Play*. Glasgow, Fontana.

George, V. and Wilding, P. (1985) *Ideology and social welfare*. London, Routledge and Kegan Paul.

Ghayle, A. and Pascal, C. (1988) *Four year old children in reception classrooms: participant perceptions and practice*. Worcester, Worcester College Occasional Paper.

GLC Women's Comittee with the Black and Ethnic Minority Childcare Group. (1986) *Childcare Our Way*. London, GLC Women's Committee.

Gold, D. and Andres, D. (1978) 'Comparisons of adolescent children with employed and unemployed mothers', *Merrill-Palmer Quarterly*, 24, 243–54.

Goodman, M.E. (1952) *Race awareness in young children*. Cambridge, MA, Addison-Wesley.

Goutard, M. (1980) *Pre-school education in the European Community*. Paris, OECD.

Graham, H. (1985) 'Maternal deprivation' in A. Branthwaite and D. Rogers (eds), *Children growning up*. Milton Keynes, Open University Press.

Grampian Regional Council (1987) *Pre-school/primary liaison*. Aberdeen, Grampian Resources Centre.

Halsey, A.H. (ed.) (1972) *Educational Priority. No 1: EPA problems and policies*. London, HMSO.

Hamilton, D. (1984) 'First days at school' in S. Delamont (ed.), *Readings on interaction in the classroom*. London, Methuen.

Hannon, P.W. and Cuckle, P. (1984) 'Involving parents in the teaching of reading', *Educational Research*, 26, 1, 7–13.

Harlow, H.F. (1961) 'The development of affectional patterns in infant monkeys' in B.M. Foss (ed.), *Determinants of infant behaviour*, Vol. 2, London, Methuen.

Hartley, D. (1980) 'Sex differences in the infant school: definitions and theories', *British Journal of Sociology of Education*. 1, 1.

Heaslip, P. (1985) 'The training and roles of nursery staff', *TACTYC*, 5, 2.

Heaslip, P. (1987) 'Does the glass slipper fit Cinderella?: nursery teachers and their training' in M.M. Clark (ed.). *Roles, responsibilities and relationships in the education of the young child*. Birmingham, University of Birmingham Occasional Publication no. 13.

Heaslip, P. (1988) *Education of Children under five*, 2, Session 1988–89 HC30–II, London, HMSO.

Hirst, P.H. (1969) 'The logic of curriculum', *Journal of Curriculum Studies*, 1, 2, 142–58.

Hogg, C. (1989) 'Daycare – the unmet needs' in M. Kozak (ed.), *Daycare for kids. A parents' survival guide*. London, Daycare Trust.

Holt, J. (1969) *How children fail*. Harmondsworth, Penguin.

Hough, J. (1984) *A study of sex differentiation in the first year of schooling*. CERD, University of Lancaster.

House of Commons Select Committee (Education, Science and Arts) (1986) *Achievement in primary schools*. London, HMSO.

House of Commons Select Committee (Education, Science and Arts) (1989) *Educational provision for the under fives*. London, HMSO.

Hoyles, M. (1979) *Changing childhood*. London, Writers and Readers.

Hughes, M. (1978) 'Selecting pictures of another person's view', *British Journal of Educational Psychology*. 48, 210–19.

Hughes, M., Mayall, B., Moss, P., Perry, J., Petrie, P. and Pinkerton, G. (1980) *Nurseries now*. Harmondsworth, Penguin.

Huston, A. (1983) 'Sex-typing' in E.M. Hetherington (ed.), *Handbook of child psychology*, Vol. 3. New York, Wiley.

Hutt, C. (1972) *Males and females*. Harmondsworth, Penguin.

Hutt, C. (1979) *Play in the under fives: form, development and function*. New York, Brunner/Mazel.

Hutt, S.J., Tyler, S., Hutt, C. and Christopherson, H. (1989) *A natural history of the preschool: exploration, play and learning*. London, Routledge.

ILEA (1981) *Education in a multiethnic society. An aide-memoire for the inspectorate*. London, ILEA.

ILEA (1982) *Pre-school provision in an area of Lewisham*. London, ILEA Research and Statistics.

ILEA (1985a) *Educational opportunities for all?* (Fish Report). London, ILEA.

ILEA (1985b) *Improving primary schools*. (Thomas Report). London, ILEA.

ILEA (1986a) *Primary matters*. London, ILEA.

ILEA (1986b) *Nursery rhyme or reason*. London, ILEA.

Isaacs, S. (1929) *The nursery years*. London, Routledge and Kegan Paul.

Isaacs, S. (1954) *The educational value of the nursery school*. London, BAECE.

Jackson, B. (1979) *Starting school*. London, Croom Helm.

Jackson, B. (1984) *Fatherhood*. London, Allen & Unwin.

Jackson, B. and Jackson, S. (1979) *Childminder*. London, Routledge and Kegan Paul.

Jackson, S. (1987) *The education of children in care*. Bristol, University of Bristol Occasional Paper.

Jensen, A.R. (1969) 'How much can we boost IQ and scholastic achievement?', *Harvard Educational Review*, 39, 1–123.

Jensen, J., Hagen, E. and Reddy, C. (1988) *Feminisation of the labour force*. Cambridge, Polity Press.

Joly, D. (1986) *The opinions of Mirpuri parents in Saltley, Birmingham, about their children's schooling*. Coventry, University of Warwick, CRER.

Jowett, S. and Sylva, K. (1986) 'Does kind of preschool matter?', *Educational Research*, 28, 1.

Kelly, A., Alexander, J., Azam, U., Bretherton, C., Burgess, G., Dorney, A., Gold, J., Leahy, C., Sharpley, A. and Spanley, L. (1986) 'Gender roles at home and schools' in L. Burton (ed.), *Girls into maths can go*. London, Holt, Rinehart and Winston.

Kessler, S. and McKenna, W. (1985) *Gender: an ethnomethodological approach*. Chicago, University of Chicago.

King, R.A. (1978) *All things bright and beautiful?* Chichester, Wiley.

Kuczaj, S.A. (1983) *Crib speech and language play*. New York. Springer.

Lally, M. (1989) *The National Curriculum and education of children aged 3 to 8*. London, NCB.

Lamb, M. (ed.) (1982) *The role of the father in child development*. New York, Wiley.

Lazar, I. and Darlington, R. (1982) Lasting effects of early education, *Monographs of the Society for Research in Child Development*. 47, Parts 1 and 2.

Lee, L. (1959) *Cider with Rosie*. London, Hogarth Press.

Liang, H. and Shapiro, J. (1983) *Son of the Revolution*. London, Chatto and Windus.

Light, P. (1979) *The development of social sensitivity*. Cambridge, Cambridge University Press.

Little, A. (1986) 'Educational inequalities: race and class' in R. Rogers (ed.), *Education and social class*. London, Falmer.

Lloyd, B. (1987) 'Social representations of gender' in J. Bruner and H. Haste (eds), *Making sense*. London, Methuen.

Lloyd, I. (1983) 'The aims of early childhood education', *Educational Review*, 35, 2, 121–5.

London Borough of Lewisham (1983) *An anti-racist approach to the care of under fives*. London, Borough of Lewisham.

Long, F. and Garduque, L. (1987) 'Continuity between home and family daycare' in D.L. Peters and S. Kontos (eds), *Continuity and discontinuity in childcare*. Norwood, NJ, Ablex.

Lubeck, S. (1985) *Sandbox society*. London, Falmer.

Lunt, I. (1983) 'Assessment of cognitive development' in S. Meadows (ed.), *Developing thinking*. London, Methuen.

Lynn, R. (1988) *Educational Achievement in Japan*. London, Macmillan.

Macbeth, A. (1984) *The child between: a report of school–family relations in the countries of the European Economic Community*. Brussels, Commission of the EC.

Maccoby, E.E. and Jacklin, C.N. (1974) *The psychology of sex differences*. Stanford, Stanford University Press.

MacLeod, F. (1985) *Parents in partnership: involving Muslim parents in their children's education*. Coventry, CEDC.

Main, M. and Weston, D.R. (1981) 'The quality of the toddler's relationship to mother and to father', *Child development*, 52, 932–40.

Martin, J. and Roberts, C. (1984) *Women and employment: a lifetime perspective. The report of the 1980 DE/OPCS women and employment survey*. London, HMSO.

May, N. and Ruddock, J. (1983) *Sex stereotyping and the early years of schooling*. Centre for Applied Research in Education, University of East Anglia.

Mayall, B. and Petrie, P. (1977) *Childminding and day nurseries: what kind of care?* London, Heinemann/London University Institute of Education.

McGarrigle, J. and Donaldson, M. (1974) 'Conservation accidents', *Cognition*, 3, 341–50.

McGill, L. (1986) 'Outdoor play' in ILEA, *Primary matters*. London, ILEA.

McMillan, M. (1914) 'The Schools of tomorrow'. *The Christian Commonwealth*, 21 January 1914.

McMillan, M. (1930) *The nursery school*. London, Dent.

Mead, M. (1943) *Coming of age in Samoa*. Harmondsworth, Penguin.

Meadows, S. (1986) *Understanding child development*. London, Hutchinson.

Meadows, S. and Cashdan, A. (1988) *Helping children learn: contributions to a cognitive curriculum*. London, David Fulton.

Meehan, E. (1985) *Women's rights at work*. London, Macmillan.

Milner, D. (1983) *Children and race ten years on*. London, Ward Lock Educational.

Ming, T. (1984) *Mother tongue maintenance*. London, CRE.

Ministry of Health and Ministry of Education (1945) *Nursery provision for children under five*. Circular 221/45. London, HMSO.

Minuchin, S. (1974) *Families and Family Therapy*. London, Tavistock.

Moore, E. and Sylva, K. (1984) 'A survey of under fives record-keeping in Britain', *Educational Research*, 26, 2, 115–20.

Moore, E. and Smith, T. (1987) *High/Scope Report 2 – One year on*. Oxford, Oxford University Dept. of Social and Administrative Studies.

Morgan, D.H.J. (1988) 'Socialisation and the family: change and diversity' in M. Woodhead and A. McGrath (eds), *Family, school and society*. London, Hodder and Stoughton/Open University.

Mortimore, J. and Blackstone, T. (1982) *Disadvantage and education*. London, Heinemann.

Mortimore, J. and Mortimore, P. (1985) 'Benign or malignant? The effects of institutions', *Child Care, Health and Development*, 11, 267–80.

Moss, P. (1988) *Childcare and equality of opportunity*. London, European Commission.

Moss, P. (1989) 'Employment, parenthood and gender' in V. Williams (ed.), *Babies in daycare*. London, The Daycare Trust.

Moyles, J. (1988) 'Does the National Curriculum mean the end of child-centred learning?' *Child Education* 65, 11.

Moyles, J. (1989) *Just playing? The role and status of play in early childhood education*. Milton Keynes, Open University Press.

Mullan, B. (1987) *Are mothers really necessary?* London, Boxtree.

Mullin, B., Morgan, V. and Dunn, S. (1986) *Gender differentiation in infant classes*. Coleraine, Faculty of Education, University of Ulster.

Murphy, H.F. (1980) 'Staff behaviour in nursery school – an observational study' *Scottish Educational Review*. 12, 2, 99–107.

Murphy, H.F. and Wilkinson, J.E. (1982) 'Cognitive socialisation of 4 year old children in nursery school', *Child Care, Health and Development*, 8, 4, 203–17.

NAHT (1987) *Early Years Education, Provision from Age 3 to 5*. Haywards Heath, NAHT.

NAPE (1986) 'A statement of policy: under fives in infant classes', *NAPE*, Autumn.

NCB (1987) *NCB Curriculum Pack – Trial version*. London, NCB.

NCVO (1986) *Policy analysis unit report*. London, NCVO.

NCVO (1987) *The use of the community programme in health and social care*. London, NCVO.

Nelson, K. (1986) *Event knowledge: structure and function in development*. Hillsdale, NJ, Erlbaum.

Neutstatter, A. (1987) 'Paying a high price for liberation', *The Guardian*, 22 December.

New, C. and David, M. (1985) *For the children's sake*. Harmondsworth, Penguin.

Newson, J. and Newson, E. (1965) *Patterns of infant care*. Harmondsworth, Penguin.

Nisbet, J. and Shucksmith, J. (1986) *Learning strategies*. London, Routledge.

O'Connor, M. (1975) 'The nursery school environment', *Developmental Psychology*, 11, 5, 556–61.

Oakley, A. (1974) *The sociology of housework*. Oxford, Martin Robertson.

Oakley, A. (1987) *Social welfare and the position of women*. London, Thomas Coram Research Unit Occasional and Working Papers.

OPCS (1989) *Population projections*. London, HMSO.

Osborn, A.F. and Milbank, J.E. (1987) *The effects of early education*. Oxford, Clarendon Press.

Palkovitz, R. (1987) 'Consistency and stability in the family microsystem environment' in D.L. Peters and S. Kontos (eds), *Continuity and discontinuity in childcare*. Norwood, NJ, Ablex.

Parry, M. and Archer, H. (1974) *Pre-school education*. London, Schools Council/ Macmillan Educational.

Pepler, D.J. and Rubin, K.H. (1982) (eds), *The play of children: current theory and research*. Basel, Karger.

Peters, R.S. (1966) *Ethics and education*. London, Allen & Unwin.

Piaget, J. (1951) *Play, dreams and imitation in childhood*. London, Routledge and Kegan Paul.

Pole, K. (1987) 'Still not far enough...', *AUT woman*, 11, Summer.

Policy Analysis Unit (1986) *Voluntary Organisations and childcare: issues and challenges*. London, NCVO.

Pollard, A. (1985) *The social world of the primary school*. London, Holt, Rinehart and Winston.

Pollard, A. and Tann, S. (1987) *Reflective teaching in the primary school*. London, Cassell.

Postman, N. (1985) *The disappearance of childhood*. London, Comet/W.H. Allen.

Powell, D.R. (1980) 'Towards a socioecological perspective of relations between parents and care programs' in S. Kilmer (ed.), *Advances in early education and day care*, Vol. 1. Grenwich, CT, JAI Press.

PPA (1986). *Facts and figures*. London, PPA.

PPA (1987) *The MSC and under fives groups. A survey by the PPA*. London, PPA.

Pringle, M.K. (1974) *The needs of children*. London, Hutchinson.

Pugh, G. (1987) 'Early education and day care: in search of a policy', *Journal of Educational Policy* 2, 4, 301–16.

Pugh, G. (1988) *Services for under fives: developing a co-ordinated approach.* London, NCB.

Pugh, G., Aplin, G., De'Ath, E. and Moxon, M. (1987) *Partnership in action.* London, NCB.

Pugh, G. and De'Ath, E. (1989) *Working towards partnership in the early years.* London, NCB.

Rabin, A.E. (1965) *Growing up on the Kibbutz.* New York, Springer.

Radin, N. (1972) 'Three degrees of parental involvement in a preschool programme: impact on mothers and children', *Child Development* 43, 1355–64.

Riach, L. (1989) 'Learning about parenting: adolescent girls discuss their perceptions of motherhood both from their experiences as daughters and their intentions as potential mothers', paper presented at the OMEP International Congress, London, 14 July.

Richman, N. and McGuire, J. (1988) 'Institutional characteristics and staff behaviour in day nurseries', *Children and Society*, 2, 2 138–51.

Richman, N., Stevenson, J. and Graham, P.J. (1982) *Pre-school to school: a behavioural study.* London, Academic Press.

Riley, D. (1983) *War in the nursery: theories of the child and mother.* London, Virago.

Robinson, E.J. and Robinson, W.P. (1982) 'The advancement of children's verbal referential communication skills: the role of metacognitive guidance', *International Journal of Behavioural Development*, 5, 329–55.

Rosen, S. (1986) 'The People's Republic of China: education during the world recession: the paradox of expansion' in F.M. Wirt and G. Harmann (eds), *Education, recession and the world village.* London, Falmer.

Rubenstein, J.L. and Howes, C. (1983) 'Socio-emotional development of toddlers in day care', *Advances in early education and care*, 3, 13–46.

Rubery, J. (1988) *Women and recession.* London, Routledge and Kegan Paul.

Rubin, Z. (1980) *Children's friendships.* Cambridge, MA, ABT Associates.

Rubin, Z., Proveszano, F.J. and Luri, A.Z. (1974) 'The eye of the beholder: parents' views on sex of newborns', *American Journal of Orthopsychiatry*, 44, 512–19.

Ruopp, R., Ravers, J., Glantz, F. and Coelen, C. (1979) *Children at the centre.* Cambridge, MA, ABT Associates.

Rutter, M. (1981) *Maternal deprivation reassessed*, 2nd edn. Harmondsworth, Penguin.

Rutter, M. and Madge, N. (1976) *Cycles of disadvantage.* London, Heinemmann.

Rutter, M., Maughan, B., Mortimore, P. and Ouston, J. (1979) *Fifteen Thousand Hours.* London, Open Books.

Saltz, E. and Brodie, J. (1982) 'Pretend play training in childhood: a review and critique' in D.J. Pepler and K.H. Rubin (eds), *The play of children: current theory and research.* Basel, Karger.

Sarup, M. (1986) *The politics of multiracial education.* London, Routledge and Kegan Paul.

Scarr, S. and Dunn, J. (1987) *Mother care/other care.* Harmondsworth, Penguin.

Schaffer, R. (1977) *Mothering.* London, Fontana/Open Books.

Schools Council (1981) *The practical curriculum*. London, Schools Council.

Schweinhart, L.J. and Weikart, D.P. (1980) *Young children grow up: the effects of the Perry Preschool Programme on youth through age 15*. Ypsilanti, Monograph of the High/Scope Educational Research Foundation. No. 7.

Schweinhart, L.J., Weikart, D.P. and Larner, M.B. (1986) 'Consequences of three preschool curriculum models through age 15' *Early Childhood Research Quarterly*, 1, 15–45.

Sestini, E. (1987) 'The quality of learning experiences for four year olds in nursery and infant classes' in NFER/SCDC Seminar Report, *Four year olds in school*. Slough, NFER/SCDC.

Sharp, C. (1987) 'Starting school at four', *Child Education*, August.

Sharp, R. and Green, A. (1975) *Education and social control*. London, Routledge and Kegan Paul.

Shinman, S (1981) *A chance for every child*. London, Tavistock.

Shorter, E. (1975) *The making of the modern family*. New York, Basic Books.

Smilansky, S. (1968) *The effects of sociodramatic play on disadvantaged preschool children*. New York, Wiley.

Smith, A.B. (1987) 'Recent developments in early childhood "Educare" in New Zealand', *Revue Internationale de L'Enfance Préscolaire*, 19, 2, 33–44.

Smith, P.K. (ed.) (1986) *Children's Play: Research, development and practical applications*. New York, Gordon and Breach.

Smith, P.K. (1988) 'The relevance of fantasy play for development in young children' in A. Cohen and L. Cohen (eds), *Early education: the preschool years*. London, PCP.

Smith, P.K. and Connolly, K.J. (1980) *The ecology of preschool behaviour*. Cambridge, Cambridge University Press.

Smith, P.K. and Sydall, S. (1978) 'Play and non-play tutoring in preschool children. Is it play or the tutoring which matters?' *British Journal of Educational Psychology*, 48, 315–25.

Smith, T. (1975) 'The Red House Project' in G. Smith (ed), *Educational priority Vol. 4. The West Riding Project*. London, HMSO.

Smith, T. (1980) *Parents and preschool*. London, Grant McIntyre.

Solomon, J. (1987) *Holding the reins*. London, Fontana.

Southwell, S. (1984) 'Racial and cultural awareness in early childhood', *TACTYC*, 4, 2.

Speekman Klass, C. (1986) *The autonomous child*. London, Falmer Press.

Spender, D. (1986) 'Some thought on the power of mathematics' in L. Burton (ed.), *Girls into maths can go*. London, Holt, Rinehart and Winston.

Spender, D. and Sarah, E. (eds) (1980) *Learning to lose: sexism in education*. London, Women's Press.

Stallibrass, A. (1975) *The self-respecting child*. Harmondsworth, Penguin.

Steedman, C. (1986) *Landscape for a good woman*. London, Virago.

Steedman, C. (1988) 'The mother made conscious: the historical development of a primary school pedagogy' in M. Woodhead and A. McGrath (eds), *Family, school and society*. London, Hodder and Stoughton/Open University.

Stenhouse, L. (1975) *An introduction to curriculum research and development.* London, Heinemann.

Stern, D. (1977) *The first relationship: infant and mother.* London, Fontana/Open Books.

Stevenson, C. (1987) 'The young four year old in nursery and infant classes: challenges and constraints' in NFER/SCDC Seminar Report, *Four year olds in school.* London, NFER/SCDC.

Stone, M. (1981) *The education of the black child.* London, Fontana.

Sutherland, M. (1988) *Theory of education.* London, Longman.

Sutton-Smith, B. (ed.) (1979) *Play and learning.* New York, Gardner Press.

Sylva, K. (1977) 'Play and learning' in B. Tizard and D. Harvey (eds), *The biology of play.* London, SIMP Heinemann.

Sylva, K., Bruner J.S. and Genova, P. (1976) 'The role of play in the problem-solving of children 3–5 years old' in J.S. Bruner, A. Jolly and K. Sylva (eds), *Play: its role in development and evolution.* Harmondsworth, Penguin.

Sylva, K., Roy, C. and Painter, M. (1980) *Childwatching at playgroup and nursery school.* London, Grant McIntyre.

Sylva, K., Smith, T. and Moore, E. (1986) *Final report of High/Scope training programme.* Oxford, Oxford University.

Taylor, D.C. (1969) 'Differential rates of cerebral maturation between sexes and betwen hemispheres', *Lancet*, 19 July, 140–2.

Taylor, M.J. (1981) *Caught between. A review of research into the education of pupils of West Indian origin.* Windsor, NFER-Nelson.

Taylor, P.H., Exon, G. and Holley, B. (1972) *A study of nursery education.* London, Schools Council.

TES (1988a) 'Going private', *Times Educational Supplement*, 29 April.

TES (1988b) 'Test them at five', *Times Educational Supplement*, 20 May.

TES (1989) 'Support for "tests" at five' *Times Educational Supplement*, 3 March.

Thomas, V. (1973) 'Children's use of language in the nursery', *Educational Research*, 15; 3, 209–16.

Thorburn, I. (1987) 'New start for under fives' *Child Education*, February.

Tilly, L.A. and Scott, J.W. (1987) *Women, work and family.* London, Methuen.

Tizard, B. (1975) 'Varieties of residential nursery experience' in J. Tizard, I. Sinclaire and R.V.G. Clarke (eds), *Varieties of residential experience.* London, Routledge and Kegan Paul.

Tizard, B., Philps, J and Plewis, I. (1976) 'Staff behaviour in preschool centres',

Tizard, B. (1986) *The care of the young children.* London, University of London Institute of Education/Thomas Coram Residential Unit.

Tizard, B., Blatchford, P., Burke, J., Farquhar, C. and Plewis, I. (1988) *Young children at school in the inner city.* Hove, Lawrence Erlbaum.

Tizard, B. and Hughes, M. (1984) *Young children learning.* London, Fontana.

Tizzard, B., Mortimore, J. and Birchell, B. (1981) *Involving parents in nursery and infant schools.* London, Grant McIntyre.

Tizard, B., Philps, J. and Plewis, I. (1976) 'Staff behaviour in preschool centres', *Journal of Child Psychology and Psychiatry*, 17, 21–33.

Tizard, J. and Tizard, B. (1983) 'The institution as an environment for development in child development and social policy' in A.D.B. Clarke and B. Tizzard (eds), *The Life and Work of Jack Tizzard*. London, British Psychological Society.

Tomlinson, J.R.G. (1986) 'The coordination of services for the under fives', *TACTYC*, 7, 1, Autumn.

Tomlinson, S. (1980) *Home and School in Multicultural Britain*. London, Batsford.

Torkington, K. (1986) 'Involving parents in the primary curriculum' in M. Hughes (ed.), *Involving parents in the primary curriculum*. Exeter, Exeter University Occasional Paper, Perspectives no. 24.

Tough, J. (1976) *Listening to children talking*. London, Ward Lock.

Triseliotis, J.P. (1976) 'Immigrants of Mediterranean origin', *Child Care, Health and Development*, 2, 365–78.

TUC, (1976) *The under-fives*. London, TUC.

Tucker, N. (1977) *What is a child?* London, Open Books.

Turner, I.F. and Green, R.V. (1977) 'Stated intention and executive practice in a traditional preschool programme', *Research in Education*, 18, 35–44.

Tyler, S. (1979) *Keele preschool assessment guide*. Windsor, NFER.

Tyler, S. (1988) 'Play in relation to the National Curriculum', paper presented to the Teaching Studies Section and Play Matters Conference – Play and community, West Sussex Institute of Higher Education, October 1988.

Unesco (1980) *International Yearbook of Education*. Geneva, Unesco.

Van der Eyken, W. (1982) *The Education of Three-to-Eight-Year-Olds in Europe in the Eighties*. Windsor, NFER-Nelson.

Van der Eyken, W. (1987) *The DHSS Under Fives Initiative 1983–87*. Bristol, University Institute of Child Health.

VOLCUF (1986) *A Guide to Anti-racist Childcare Practice*. London, VOLCUF.

Vygotsky, L.S. (1962) *Thought and Language*. Cambridge, MA, MIT Press.

Vygotsky, L.S. (1978) *Mind in Society: The Development of Higher Psychological Processes*. Cambridge, MA, Harvard University Press.

Walden, R. and Walkerdine, V. (1982) *Girls and Mathematics: the Early Years*. London, Bedford Way.

Walker, A. (1955) *Pupils' School Records*. London, Newnes Educational Publishing Company for NFER.

Walkerdine, V. (1982) 'From context to text: a psychosemiotic approach to abstract thought' in M. Beveridge (ed.), *Children Thinking Through Language*. London, Arnold.

Walkerdine V. (1984) 'Developmental psychology and child-centred pedagogy' in J. Henriques, W. Holloway, C. Urwin, C. Venn and V. Walkerdine *Changing the Subject: Psychology, Social Regulation and Subjectivity*. London, Methuen.

Walkerdine, V. (1985) 'Child development and gender: the making of teachers and learners in nursery classrooms' in C. Adelman, B. Perry, H. Silver, V. Walkerdine and M. Willes, *Early Childhood Education: History, Policy and Practice*. Reading, Bulmershe.

Wall, W.D. (1947) 'The opinions of teachers on parent-teacher cooperation', *British Journal of Educational Psychology*, 17, 2, 97–113.

Wallace, F. (1985) 'The aims of nursery education as perceived by head teachers of nursery schools and teachers with posts of responsibility for reception children in large primary schools', unpublished dissertation for M.Ed (Ed Psych.) University of Birmingham.

Ward, P. (1982) 'Parental involvement in preschool provision: the views of parents and staff of children in nursery schools and playgroups', unpublished MA thesis, University of Keele.

Watt, J. (1977) *Cooperation in Preschool Education*. London, SSRC.

Watt, J. (1987) 'Continuity in early· education' in M.M. Clark (ed.), *Roles, Responsibilities and Relationships in the Education of the Young Child*. Birmingham, Birmingham University Educational Review Occasional Publication no. 13.

Webb, L. (1974) *Purpose and Practice in Nursery Education*. Oxford, Basil Blackwell.

Webb, N.B. (1984) *Preschool Children with Working Parents: an Analysis of Attachment*. New York, University Press of America.

Wedge, P. and Prosser, H. (1973) *Born to Fail?* London, Arrow Books.

Weikart, D., Rogers, L., Adcock, C. and McClelland, D. (1971) *The Cognitively Oriented Curriculum*. Urbana, Illinois and Washington DC, Educational Resources Information.

Wells, G. (1985) *Language Development in the Preschool Years*. Cambridge, Cambridge University Press.

Wells, I. and Burke, S. (1988) *Nursery Questions and Teachers' Answers*. Report 8, Research and consultancy service, Northern Ireland Council for Educational Research.

Whitebrook, M., Howes, C., Darrah, R. and Friedman, J. (1982) 'Caring for the care-givers: staff burn-out in child-care' in L. Katz (ed.), *Current Topics in Early Childhood Education*, Vol. IV. Norwood NJ, Ablex.

Whiting, B. (ed.) (1963) *Six Cultures – Studies of Childrearing*. New York, Wiley.

Whyte, J. (1983) *Beyond the Wendy House: Sex Role Stereotyping in Primary Schools*. London, Longman/Schools Council.

Wicks, M. (1988) *Families and the State: Section 2. Family Change and the Social Policy Agenda*. London, Family Policy Studies Centre.

Widdowson, F. (1986) ' "Educating teacher": women and elementary teaching in London' in L. Davidoff and B. Westover (eds), *Our Work, Our Lives, Our Words*. London, Macmillan.

Widlake, P. (1986) *Reducing Educational Disadvantage*. Milton Keynes, Open University Press.

Willes, M. (1983) *Children into Pupils*. London, Routledge and Kegan Paul.

Winnicott, D.W. (1964) *The Child, the Family and the Outside World*. Harmondsworth, Penguin.

Wirt, F.M. and Harmann, G. (1986) *Education, Recession and the World Village*. London, Falmer Press.

Witcher, H. (1985) 'Personal and professional: a feminist approach' in J. Whyte, R. Deem, L. Kant and M. Cruickshank (eds), *Girl Friendly Schooling*. London, Methuen.

Witherspoon, S. (1988) 'Interim report: a woman's work' in R. Jowell, S. Witherspoon and L. Brook (eds), *British Social Attitudes: The 5th Report*. London, Gower Press.

Wood, D. (1986) 'Aspects of teaching and learning' in M. Richards and P. Light (eds), *Children of Social Worlds*. Cambridge, Polity Press.

Wood, D. (1988) *How Children Think and Learn*. Oxford, Basil Blackwell.

Wood, D., Bruner, J.S. and Ross, G. (1976) 'The role of tutoring in problem solving', *Journal of Child Psychology and Psychiatry*, 17, 2, 89–100.

Wood, D., McMahon, L. and Cranstoun, Y. (1980) *Working with Under Fives*. London, Grant McIntyre.

Woodhead, M. (1976) *Intervening in Disadvantage*. Windsor, NFER–Nelson.

Woodhead, M. (1979) 'Preschool provision in Western Europe' in Council of Europe and NFER, *Young Children in European Societies in the Eighties: From Birth to Eight*. Windsor, NFER–Nelson.

Woodhead, M. (1985) 'Preschool provision has long-term effects: but can they be generalised?' *Oxford Review of Education*, 11, 2, 133–55.

Woodhead, M. (1989) 'School starts at five . . . or four years old? The rationale for changing admission policies in England and Wales', *Journal of Education Policy*, 4, 1, 1–21.

Yarrow, L. (1967) 'The development of focused relationships during infancy' in J. Hellmuth (ed.) *The Exceptional Infant*. Vol. 1. The Normal Infant. Seattle, Special Child Publications.

Zigler, E.F. (1987) 'Formal Schooling for four year olds? No.' *American Psychologist*, 42, 3, 254–60.

Index